MW01146474

Whales with Fur

How to train any animal using dolphin training techniques

Whales with Fur

How to train any animal using
dolphin training techniques

Pete Davey

Ocean Publishing
Flagler Beach, Florida

Whales with Fur

How to train any animal using
dolphin training techniques

By Pete Davey

Published by:
Ocean Publishing
Post Office Box 1080
Flagler Beach, FL 32136-1080
orders@ocean-publishing.com
www.ocean-publishing.com

ISBN, print ed.........................0-9717641-5-8
LCCN...................................2004100053

Printed and bound in the United States of America

Dedication

This book is dedicated with great love to Jody and our greatest training challenges –

Kelsey, Ty, Sam and Kate.

Acknowledgments

Humans: Dad, Mom, Mark, Kim, Steve, Ken, Lisa, Bill, Chip, Greg, Mega, and the rest of the gang (they've been stuck with me since 1990…they know who they are)

Places: Mystic Aquarium, Mystic, Connecticut; Shedd Aquarium, Chicago, Illinois; Ocean Journey, Denver, Colorado; Marineland of Florida

Critters: Skipper, Hank, Kodiak, Sira, Quitz, Katrl, Piquet, Kri, Tique, Bulea, Naya, Puiji, Immi, Naluark, #4, #6, Ariel, Esther, Orange, Kachemak, Nuka, Chenik, Nikishka, Kenai, Bali, Java, Malu, Gracie, Taylor, Haley, Blue, Slater, Gunnison, Betty, Dazzle, Phebe, Casique, Alvin, Chubby, Sunny, Pebbles, Roxy, Lilly, and Nellie... and many others.

Table of Contents

Foreword

I've been around animals all my life—both domestic and wild. One thing I've learned is that they are all different, not only as species, but as individuals, as well. And even though animals can be so different, in my travels and through all my experiences with animals, I've noticed a common thread. One of the best ways to take care of any animal is through training—training is just teaching, whether for physical and mental stimulation, or for the best care of the animal. Animal training, although pioneered through amazing work with dolphins and whales, is now used successfully with many species of animals. In fact, training programs are becoming common at many zoos.

So even though each animal is unique as a species, and even each individual can be unique, one can look at working with the animals in a consistent, clear manner. This is exactly what *Whales with Fur* is all about.

Pete Davey has trained whales and dolphins for several years, and used the same training approach for tigers, otters, and other animals. And now you can learn how to use it, as well! Pete discusses training approaches in a fun way that will make your relationship with your pet much happier and healthier.

It is imperative that your pet knows what you want—and don't want—from it. This is an important relationship and your pet should not go from day to day with mixed messages that don't make sense. So, enjoy **Whales with Fur** and soon you'll be enjoying everything you've wanted from your pet—and maybe even more!

Jack Hanna,
Director Emeritus, Columbus Zoo
and Host of TV's "Animal Adventures"

Introduction

OK, so what are "Whales with Fur"? That's a really good question. Actually, whales do have hair, but it falls off before birth. The title refers to using whale and dolphin training techniques for any animal and basically looking at your animals as "whales with fur" when you train them.

Marine mammal trainers, like me, have always said that our training methodology works for anything and everything. You just adjust it a little bit for whatever species you are working with.

I had the opportunity to effectively demonstrate this with an entire training program I designed around mostly non-marine mammals. It worked rather well. And it can work for you, too! Forget whether it is a dog, or cat, or horse, or pot-bellied pig in front of you – just look at them as "Whales with Fur."

There are several very common questions we hear when we work with dolphins and whales. The first is always, "How do I get your job?" But, the second most asked question is, "How do you guys do that?" This is followed by, "Why can't I do that with Fluffy?" *(Naming your pet Fluffy might have something to do with his unwillingness to do stuff for you!).*

Well, it's really pretty simple. Keep in mind we work with our animals all day long, seven days a week, doing anywhere from 2-12 training sessions a day. If you knew the basics, and put in the time, even Fluffy would look pretty darn sharp when you say "sit."

I can't schedule your time for you, but we can talk about some of the basic methods that are very effective in whale and dolphin training, and work just as well with Fluffy. The trick is to know these basics, and again, to simply look at your animal or animals as "Whales with Fur."

Pete with Chubby

Chapter 1: What do I know?

So who am I to tell you that you can train your animal if you treat it like a "whale with fur"? That's a great question. You should do whatever you feel is best for your Fluffy *(Again, you may have already missed the boat when you named him)*. Of course, you can do that with anything, but let's say you cut off your finger. I suggest finding a doctor rather than stitching it back on yourself.

When working with animals, especially ones you have emotional ties to, it certainly can't hurt to get advice from someone with some background and experience in animal training. So let me fill you in on my background and experience, and then we'll talk about working with your own little whale with fur *(and we're going to say good-bye to Fluffy)*.

I'll make the biography short and sweet, and you'll find a few pictures of some of the training techniques and animals along the way. Ready for a picture show? Don't fall asleep!

Mystic, Connecticut

One of the keys to getting a job as a trainer is "right time, right place." In 1988, I sent out about 30 letters to aquariums around the country, saying how much I wanted to be a dolphin trainer *(It's a pretty funny letter - I have it laminated!)* Most return letters said, "Sorry, don't call us and we won't call you." One place responded that it had an opening in visitor services, and I think I'm still the only person in history to show up in a full suit and tie for an interview for a part time position paying minimum wage! But I got the job as a V.I.P. (visitor information personnel).

I volunteered two full days per week with the seals and sea lions *(Tip number two in getting a job as a trainer – volunteer!)* and five weeks later I was hired for an open position in Exhibits and Husbandry. My title was "seal island aquarist." We took care of and trained 11 sea lions, an elephant seal, 15 northern fur seals, four gray seals, and 10 harbor seals.

Just to make it interesting, we added African black-footed penguins to the mix. There were only three of us on the seal island staff, so we learned on the job, and most of the training actually was done by the sea lions *(They trained me!)*.

It was a great way to break into the field, and a lot of fun. But I still wanted those dolphins!

Chicago, Illinois

After 18 months with seals and seal lions, I got dolphins. In June 1990, I was hired as part of a brand-new staff for an oceanarium being built at the Shedd Aquarium in Chicago. Those of us on the original staff were part of building a program from scratch. We got a chance to do everything! It was a blast being part of the program from day one and helping to build what is one of the best oceanarium programs in the country today. And I finally had dolphins - and whales! *(Actually, dolphins are just little whales.)*

Whales with Fur

In my almost nine years at Shedd, I worked with beluga whales, Pacific white-sided dolphins, harbor seals, northern sea otters and more penguins.

I worked for two of the best animal trainers in the business, and learned something from them every day. Eventually, after being part of a team building a new program, I wanted to see if I could build my own program. There are extremely few opportunities to do that, but eventually one came along.

Denver, Colorado

In late 1998, I was given a chance to build that program at Colorado's Ocean Journey, a new aquarium set to open in Denver in 1999. So I picked up my family and moved to Denver.

Using all the training I had learned over the years with whales and dolphins, I designed and built a program from the ground up. But there was one small problem - no whales or dolphins! Instead, our animals were river otters, sea otters and Sumatran tigers.

But it's hard to teach a trainer new tricks, so the program was designed to be exactly as it would be if we did have dolphins and whales. At first, most of the trainers I hired had a marine mammal background. As the program progressed, and visiting professionals would ask about our approach, I ended up with the best way to explain it. I would simply tell them: "Basically, we look at all of our animals as whales with fur." In fact, I ended up presenting a paper on how we created our training program. It was well received by the training community and it was titled *(Have you guessed yet?)* "Whales with Fur."

This is what gave me the idea that maybe others would be interested in trying it out on their animals. So to sum up, over the past 16 years, I have worked with and trained harbor seals, gray seals, elephant seals, northern fur seals, California sea lions, four different kinds of penguins, beluga whales, Pacific white-sided dolphins, northern sea otters, southern sea otters, North American river otters, Sumatran tigers, bottlenose dolphins, and a few assorted others.

Today - St. Augustine, Florida

In April 2003, after trying out dolphin training methods on all these different animals, I figured what the heck..., how 'bout dolphins again?

I was offered the opportunity to rebuild the training programs for the very first oceanarium in the world, Marineland of Florida. It seemed like a great challenge, so I left my whales with fur, and went back to..., well, just whales! So, if you are ever in St. Augustine, stop by to see us. It's a great place, and we're making the animal training program one of the best in the country.

So, that's the background and experience that might help you with training your animals. With the picture show out of the way, why don't we move on? Let's talk about training your very own "Whales with Fur."

Chapter 2: Fluffy is really smart

"What's the smartest animal?" Boy, if I had a nickel for every time I've heard that question. Well, I'd have a lot of nickels. Look, we as a human race can barely figure out how to measure IQ among ourselves, let alone figure it out for all those animals. Animals seem to be as intelligent as they need to be.

For example, good ol' *Homo sapiens* was pretty much designed poorly in terms of physical defense. We don't have much in the way of fur, teeth, strength, speed, eyesight, scent or hearing, at least not compared to some other critters out there. So what happened? We survived anyway, and that could be due to the level of "intelligence" or logic, and ability to learn, that this woefully inadequate species had to develop just to survive.

So when you are trying to compare intelligence, at least when thinking of training, it really doesn't apply. Can a dolphin run across a field and catch a Frisbee? Or can a dog dive a mile down to find a lost object? No, and no! But, is either smarter than the other? Nope, they are just different.

This is how you want to look at working with animals. One isn't smarter or dumber or harder or easier - they are just different. Learn their individual characteristics, and know their physical attributes and limitations. *(Training a pot-bellied pig to leap up and catch a Frisbee is not a good example of considering physical attributes!)*

In other words, you can train just about anything using the same approach we have used to train dolphins and whales.

Chapter 3: Why train?

Contrary to some scuttlebutt you hear out there, we train for the animals' sake. In the training field, we train for physical exercise, mental stimulation and cooperative behaviors. The first two are basically for the well-being of the animal, which is not in its natural environment. For animals in the wild, every day is a battle for survival.

Consider survival as kind of a game - one that occupies the individual animal just about 24-hours a day. Survival is not a fun game, and if the animal loses, it does not get to start over. Survival is demanding both physically and mentally. Training animals replaces that "game" with ones that are both physically and mentally stimulating, with no adverse consequence if they don't play well.

The third reason for training is to establish cooperative behaviors. This just means we teach the animals to help us take care of them. To make a long story short, we teach the animals that going to the vet is a game and we play that game every single day, whether a vet is there or not. And those "games" include numerous veterinary or cooperative behaviors (just about any medical thing you can imagine). To the animal, it's just part of the training session.

What if your dog liked going to the vet? *(Guess what? Dogs don't know they're going; they just recognize a car ride and something that always terminates in unpleasantness.)*

One time we had to transport four dolphins from California to Illinois. We were to drive them in a truck to a plane, fly them to Chicago, load them on to a flatbed truck, drive to an aquarium, and put them in their new home.

Whales with Fur

Several months before, we started getting them to swim into stretchers, and then got them used to going for rides on a truck until the truck happened to go to the airport. The rides were made positive and when the time came to transport, they did great.

If you were to take your dog for a car ride every day or just every week, and make it fun each time, I absolutely guarantee that it won't care or even know it is going to the vet. For that matter, you can train your animals to think hanging out with the vet is fun!

As for mental stimulation and physical exercise, four 5-minute sessions a day with a dog will give it far more stimulation than one walk through the park in the morning and one at night.

So training is really all for the animal. Plus, it also helps to build that relationship of trust that is so important for both the animal and you.

Chapter 4: Learnin' the lingo

Like learning any new skill, you need to know the language before being able to understand someone who only knows how to talk in "trainer-speak." Actually, trainer talk is not idiomatic so much as it is based in the true terms of operant conditioning, and elements of psychology.

First, operant conditioning does not involve Pavlov's dogs. Second, I won't throw the scientific technical definitions at you because they can be somewhat confusing. Instead, I'll use several common terms, which will be used throughout the book, so pay attention!

Operant Conditioning

This is basically learning by having behavior affected by its consequences. You don't want to mix this up with classical conditioning, like Pavlov's dogs salivating at the sound of a bell. That is more simple association than anything else. Skipper (our dog for many of our examples) learns to do something or not do something by the response given him during the behavior. Whatever response (which is called either reinforcement or punishment) he elicits, teaches him something.

Now, on to those responses, but first try to erase any prior conception of what the words "positive" and "negative" mean. This is not a touchy-feely self-help book.

Positive Reinforcement

The term is easy to break down. Positive does not imply happy or good; it simply means, "added." When something is given to, or added to, Skipper's environment, that would be "positive." The reinforcement part is the good part. That just means we reinforce (exactly like it sounds) a desired behavior. We increase the likelihood of that behavior happening again by adding something to the animal's environment.

For example, if a beluga whale spits in the air *(pretty common behavior)*, and you give her a handful of herring, the likelihood that the behavior will occur again increases. When you give them something they like for doing the behavior you wanted, this makes it more likely they will do that behavior again. If every time you call

Skipper he comes to you, and he gets a pat on the head when he arrives, that is positive reinforcement.

Negative Reinforcement

OK, this one is still confused by 25-year veteran dolphin trainers. It is not uncommon to hear, "We never use negative reinforcement with Skipper!" Well, actually, you do - all the time. When you called Skipper and he came? And let's say he scratched at the door to be let in? When you opened the door, you negatively reinforced him for scratching!

Negative means "subtracted" in animal training, and reinforcement means you increase the likelihood of that behavior happening again. Skipper scratched the door, and you opened it. You subtracted something he didn't like (the door) and, therefore, made it very likely he would scratch again. By subtracting the door, you increased the behavior of scratching - and that is negative reinforcement.

Now scratching is not usually a desired behavior, but that matters not at all. Many trained behaviors are not what you wanted or had any clue you were training *(Scratching, barking, whining, and jumping up on guests are usually very well trained behaviors that have been reinforced both positively and negatively over and over again - by accident!).* We'll talk about that more a little later on.

Positive Punishment

OK, most good whale trainers do not use positive punishment, but many animal owners do. It is effective, but not nearly as effective as the reinforcement side of things. Again, positive means "added" and punishment is anything likely to DECREASE a behavior happening again. Whacking Skipper because he just piddled on the rug is positive punishment **OR IS INTENDED TO BE!** Like most things, intent is not the same as the actual process.

Ask yourself, "Did I whack Skipper <u>AS</u> he was taking a nice piddle on the rug? Or, did I whack him when I found it?" A key issue in reinforcement and punishment is <u>TIMING</u>. If you find a puddle of piddle *(say that five times fast)* and call Skipper, and then you whack him one when he shows up *(regardless of whether pointing at the puddle or shoving his nose in the piddle or just assuming he understands your shouting)*, what did you just punish (positively)? You basically just told him "BAD" for coming when you called him! So you are decreasing the likelihood of him coming when you call!

But don't worry. Even the pros sometimes mess up timing. The key is to recognize timing and intent. By the way, nothing you do will make your dog understand that late punishment is for what **YOU** think it's for. He will just relate it to whatever he was doing at the moment.

Just watch dogs in a park that don't come when they are called. When they finally do show up at the frustrated owners, what usually happens? WHACK! Gee, I wonder why they don't come over when called?! Actually, that is one of the reasons positive punishment isn't very effective. Timing is thrown off by anger or emotion, and we are venting more than training *(which sounds remarkably like being a parent)*.

Negative Punishment

Sounds really bad, huh? Actually, just apply the terms. Negative is subtraction; punishment is decreasing a behavior. Grounding your teenager is negative punishment. You are subtracting privileges and hoping to decrease an unwanted behavior *(such as staying out to 4:00 a.m. with your Chevy)*.

Now, avoidance doesn't count as training. If you lock Skipper out of your bedroom *(subtracting him from hanging with you)*, and hope to decrease the behavior of him jumping on the bed, good luck. All you've done is take away his opportunity to tuck himself into the bed. It doesn't teach him anything! *(It does work, though, and making a behavior impossible to do is a very strong tool, as well. There's even a technical term for that, but I'll spare you!)*

For the most part, we will be talking about positive reinforcement. It is the simplest approach, and the easiest to use.

Reinforcer

Again, a reinforcer is something added to or removed from the environment, which increases the likelihood of a behavior happening again; that would imply something good. There are two main ways to reinforce *(actually there are lots more, but this is not a textbook)*: primary and secondary.

Primary Reinforcer

This is something the animal requires, such as food or water. You are not a primary reinforcer, no matter how much you want to be.

Food or water tends to be the most powerful type of reinforcer *(and no, you don't have to starve an animal to get it to work with you)*. Little bits of hot dog are an amazingly effective primary reinforcer for dogs.

Secondary, or conditioned, Reinforcer
These are things animals either like naturally or that we teach them to like. Skipper probably likes having his ears scratched - that is a secondary. IT IS BEST TO MAKE SURE HE LIKES IT. Skipper may like YOU scratching his head, but what about anyone else?

The best secondaries are conditioned with a primary. You know the primary is a solid reinforcer, so you pair it with a secondary and pretty soon there's an association between the ear scratching and hot dogs, and both become reinforcing.

For example, beluga whales seem to love having their tongues scratched, but do you want to be the first person they don't like doing it? We'll just call you stumpy. *(Alright, so they only have tiny little teeth, but they still have really strong jaws.)*

Bridge (or bridging stimulus)
So how do you communicate all this stuff to Skipper? Unlike your teenager, he does not, nor will he ever, speak English *(your teenager CAN, he/she just chooses not to listen to it)*. So we teach them a way to say "good job."

We actually make a **"bridge"** between the behavior and the reinforcer, which is how the teaching happens!

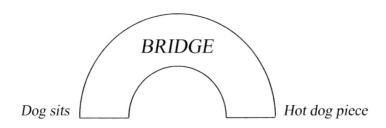

If you ask Skipper to sit, and he does, you say "good job" and that means he is going to get something tasty, or a pat on the head, etc. Guess what will happen next time you ask him to sit? He'll learn that the behavior will be accompanied by something he likes, i.e. positive reinforcement (hot dog or head pat). By linking a "bridge" (such as a dog whistle or saying "good") from the desired behavior to the reinforcement, it's a lot more concise than just trying to give Skipper a treat **exactly** at the same time he does the behavior. And if you're not exact, you won't be training the desired behavior.

Discriminative stimuli

More commonly known as an S^d (just say it like the letters…ess-dee), an S^d is just a cue. The word "SIT" is an S^d.

You show Skipper an S^d (a cue), which communicates what behavior he is supposed to do. When he does the behavior, you "bridge" (whistle) at the exact moment the behavior happens, and give him a reinforcer (hot dog, pat on the head, etc.). Don't worry; we'll go into this in more detail in a minute.

OK, got all that? I'll keep reminding you of these terms as we go along.

Pete Davey trying to keep thoughts in his head

Chapter 5: Some thoughts to keep in your head before you start...

There are some very basic steps in starting out to make your animals into little (or big) whales with fur. And there are also some key thoughts to keep in your head...

DO NOT THINK FOR THE ANIMAL

This is a big one, and my trainers hear it all the time. One of the biggest mistakes trainers make is to assume they know what the animal is thinking. YOU DON'T! What you think you are asking the animal to do, and what the animal is doing, may be totally different.

Trainers should bridge what the animal is actually doing at that moment, not what the trainer <u>hopes</u> it is doing. In other words, don't think for the animal, just work with what you see.

A great example is a trainer working with a dolphin and the dolphin is sent out to do a jump *(we call them bows)*. The trainer is thinking, "OK, I'm supposed to bridge bows." The dolphin jumps out of the water, the trainer bridges, thinking, "There, the dolphin is jumping."

OK, but how high was the jump? Did she bridge at the best height? Or at the very top of the leap? Or did you just tell the animal "good job" for coming down? Or for re-entering the water? The trainer "bridged herself" when she'd done what she was taught, rather than bridging what the animal was actually doing.

Let's get back to Skipper. You want him to sit. You ask him to sit, and he just stands in front of you wagging his tail. So you push his behind down and say "good," which is a bridge.

What did you just bridge? Perhaps you think you just bridged the dog for sitting down, but that is only in YOUR mind.

What's Skipper thinking? Most likely he's thinking, "Wow, they push on my butt, and say good job." While I don't know this for sure, I do know that is what was bridged. You may be fairly satisfied with yourself, but you bridged what YOU were thinking the dog should do, NOT what the dog was actually doing

OK, if this sounds confusing, I have debates with 20-year trainers on this all the time, so you're just as confused as the rest of us.

SET HIM UP TO SUCCEED

This just means make it easy for Skipper to learn the next step in a desired behavior. If you are trying to teach Skipper to fetch, you don't use a '57 Chevy as your retrieval item. If you are training your horse to get into a trailer, don't train the behavior using a little red wagon.

Get the idea? Now this is often confused with allowing your animal to "almost get it right." Setting Skipper up to succeed does not mean telling him good job when he ALMOST sits, but doesn't. Many new trainers will say, "I was setting him up to succeed." Actually, you were training him to "almost sit," and then stand up. Setting him up to succeed when training a "sit" would mean not doing it where he can't physically sit *(like on the edge of a cliff)*.

When a dolphin is tail-walking, bridging a "lazy" tail-walk (only a few feet out of the water) is not setting the dolphin up to succeed. It is just sloppy training. Working on tail-walks when you have the dolphin in a bigger area is setting it up to succeed (where it has the depth and distance to be able to do it).

In other words, how well or poorly Skipper does something is not how you are setting him up to succeed. Setting him up to succeed means you make it easy to accomplish the behavior and to accomplish it well. A good example would be to train Skipper to "sit" on a flat grassy surface, and where he won't fall off the top of a hill when he tries to sit. *(Training Skipper in a field full of rabbits is not setting him up to succeed.)* Or, when training a horse to go into his trailer, and using a full-size horse trailer that he is already comfortable with, is another good example of setting him up to succeed.

Bottom line: don't make it harder than it needs to be.

NEVER ASSUME YOUR ANIMAL KNOWS WHEN IT DOES SOMETHING RIGHT OR WRONG

This is amazingly uniform with owners *(including me)*. You come home and find that Skipper has eaten your slippers. Well, unless you catch him actually chewing them, there is nothing you can do. Remember TIMING? But most people yell, or smack his nose or drag him away by his collar or hit him with the tattered remains of a slipper, and the next time you come home, he acts very submissive or scared.

The next assumption is, "Oh look, he knows he did something wrong." Actually, he's just recently learned that when you come home, he gets yelled at, dragged by the collar, hit on the nose, and whacked with a slipper. How do you expect him to act? Animals learn very well. The key is what you teach them.

KEEP THOSE SESSIONS SHORT AND POSITIVE

Any time you are working with an animal, do not work too long or they *(not to mention you)* will get frustrated. If you can end with them getting a behavior right, that's best! What little lasting impression they have of the session will be positive and they will look forward to training sessions. After all, this is time spent with you, which hopefully is a reinforcer all by itself.

I find eight to ten minutes is a good time frame, and you can always cut it short on really good progress. Why keep pushing if Skipper just got it right? This can be very difficult and is one of my biggest weaknesses as a trainer. I want to train it all, and right away! But, unless you have a very good trainer's instinct as to when you have maximized the session, trying longer doesn't work well. Be patient, wait until the next session, and start from your success point.

REINFORCE DESIRED RESPONSES; IGNORE UNWANTED RESPONSES

Last, but certainly not least, this is the most basic principle of successful training. Always keep this one in the very front of your brain. If you say "good job" and give some hot dog to Skipper whenever he delivers the "desired response," he's going to end up trained on that behavior.

When you ignore things you don't want, you run no risk of accidentally reinforcing him. This goes back to thinking for the animal. You really can't be sure of what is reinforcing and what isn't, <u>but you can be sure that ignoring unwanted behavior is not reinforcing, and you won't end up accidentally training something like barking or whining</u>.

The hard part of this is those behaviors that are self-reinforcing, such as digging or chasing off after a cat. You can ignore those all you want, but Skipper will reinforce himself just by enjoying the behavior. But there are ways, through training, to get rid of undesirable behaviors as well. OK, enough training babble. Ladies and gentlemen: Start your training!

Chapter 6: Getting started on your very own whale

The very first thing you want to do is establish a positive, trusting relationship with your animal. Knowing what Skipper likes, how he works or plays with you, and his comfort level with you, is all very important. You can always bring in a consultant, but the dog doesn't know them or have the same relationship. **YOU are the best trainer for Skipper.** You just need to know what to do.

Building a relationship is half done for you. You already spend time with him; you know he likes his ears rubbed and his belly scratched. He really likes hot dogs and little bits of cheese. This is all part of building that relationship, and lots of trust. Both are key elements in being successful as a trainer.

Choose a bridge

In other words, teach your animal how you want to say "good job." You can use "good job" if you like, but it's a bit long and can't be said very concisely. Another problem with verbal bridges, such as "good," is you tend to use them all the time, even when not training, and that can be confusing and take away it's effectiveness as a bridge.

For example, if you come home after work and Skipper puts his feet up on your chest, and you say, "What a good boy, good doggy. Did you have a good day?" you just bridged him three times. And for what? Basically for jumping up on you!

Plus, you didn't reinforce him consistently for each bridge, so the bridge fades out as a training tool. My preference for a concise, easy to use bridge, and one that keeps both hands free, is an Acme dog whistle. *(And yes, both you and Skipper can hear it.)*

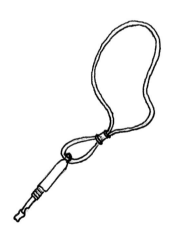

This is what I have used for any animals I have worked with. Tigers didn't mind it, horses aren't startled by it. It works for everything and, if used properly, is a very precise way to tell an animal "Good."

Choose a primary reinforcer

It is much easier to use primary reinforcers *(remember, an effective primary is food)* when you have something small, easy to carry by your side, and simple to give to Skipper. *(Peanut butter is not a good choice).*

It should be easy to eat quickly. If Skipper sits down to chew on a bone, your session is over. For a dog, I suggest small pieces of hot dog. Cut up two hot dogs into about 15 pieces each and you have a good amount for a training session. For a cat, you might try small liver treats cut in half, and for a horse, small pieces of carrot work really well.

Knowing your animal better than I, choose what it likes, and what is easy. Use that relationship you built. Some dogs might spit hot dogs right back at you, so find something else they like *(although I have yet to meet a dog that doesn't like bits of hot dog).*

The old myth you may have read about not using food in training because it is too distracting for the animal simply isn't true. If having meat chunks in a container strapped to my hip doesn't distract tigers, I doubt Skipper will have a problem.

It's also helpful to make a food container called a hip pouch *(or have your pocket get really, really yucky).* Just take a small plastic food storage container, cut a slot in each end, and put it on a belt or bungee cord. This works great and makes accessing your *(say it with me)* **primary reinforcer** very simple and at your fingertips.

Accessibility to your reinforcer is very important. If you take too long to follow up the "good job" (**bridge**) with your hot dog bits (**reinforcer**), you may end up with a frustrated animal.

Skipper doesn't really care if your jeans are too tight and you can't get your hand out of your pocket with the hot dog. He just wants the hot dog. You told him he had one coming by bridging him, and the quicker you deliver, the clearer your message is to the animal.

Now you have the foundation for getting started. Two of the first steps can be worked on at the same time.

First, it is very difficult to work with an animal that is running around a field, or asleep on the deck, so you need to establish a place to work and a way of telling Skipper that a training session is going to happen. So what we are going to do is teach Skipper about a "station" and a "bridge."

A "**station**" is basically wherever you are going to do a training session. When I was working with 11 sea lions at once, stations were places on the beach where the animals always went at the start of a session. Their training session wouldn't begin unless they first were on their "seats" (at station).

When you are working with only one animal (as I would strongly suggest), you can simply make that station wherever <u>you</u> are. *(If you and Skipper are about to start a training session, it is really helpful if he is actually there with you!)*

We'll let the hot dog bits work for us. When Skipper sees you with a little hip pouch and smells the contents, my guess is he'll come right over to see what's up. Feed him the little hot dog bits (**reinforcers**) until they run out.

Believe it or not, you are setting up your criteria for a training session. After a few sessions where you just give him several reinforcers (hot dog bits), he's going to start showing up whenever you have that bin on. This is not a concise message, but it establishes you, the trainer, as a positive place to be. Again, it's part of building that trust.

By doing this, you are also laying the groundwork for a "start of session" signal. This can be as simple as calling his name when a session is to start and having him come over (although that is a single behavior that will be useful whether you are in a training session or not), or you can do what we did in the programs I have been a part of.

We started off with a double blast of the whistle to say, "Hey, guys, time to start." At first, you are simply pairing your showing up with reinforcers with that double blast, but by pairing those two events, you are teaching Skipper that when he hears the double blast, it means a session *(with those neat little bits of meat)* is starting. Once Skipper comes over consistently, you can begin pairing the reinforcer with the bridge (your whistle).

This is the exact same concept as pairing the double blast with your coming out for a session, but the bridge will become your most important tool.

Teach the animal "the bridge"

Many folks mistakenly believe an animal knows what "good" means. Actually, you could teach a dog that "good" means "no," and "bad" means "good." The only reason Skipper slinks around with hound-dawg eyes and his tail between his legs when you say or shout "BAD" is because he associates it with something that is always paired with that word.

What do people usually do when they shout "BAD"? Their body language is very intimidating, and often a smack on the nose, rear end, or worse, is about to follow.

Skipper **learned** the word was negative by the action accompanying it. He does not speak English, so words don't have meaning to him unless we give them one. So we teach him what the bridge means ("good job") and that hearing that whistle is a very good thing. This is a really simple step.

Every time you blow the whistle (the **bridge**), give Skipper a piece of hot dog (**reinforcer**). **Not after, or before, but at exactly the same time.** In other words, you *pair* the bridge to the reinforcer.

You do this for the whole session. After two or three sessions like this, Skipper will understand that the whistle (**bridge**) means hot dog (**reinforcer**) and you have a great way of saying "good job" and telling Skipper exactly what he's doing right at exactly the right time.

But remember, timing is everything. If you are ever a little bit late or early with that bridge, you might be saying good job for something you definitely are not trying to train. At the same time, you are also teaching Skipper to stay at that station.

Perhaps you're thinking, "How do I get my dog to come to me, especially if he found a nice smelly pile of something to chew, roll in, or sniff at for several hours?" Well, you have that double blast, which means, "Hey, something really fun, involving food, is about to start."

You're trying to be as clear as possible for Skipper in telling him what you want. That double blast means, very clearly, a training session is about to begin.

Then, keep training the bridge. Each time you bridge and reinforce *(I don't need to keep saying whistle and hot dog, do I?)*, you are saying good job for calm **stationing.** Keep the session very short. Then let Skipper run around a bit, and try using your start of session S^d (cue) again (the double blast). When he runs over, bridge and reinforce, and then start your session.

If he doesn't run over right away, **DO NOT** use your double blast again (the start of session S^d). This will just desensitize him to his call to station, and he won't respond. Simply be patient and wait for him.

If he doesn't come over in a few minutes, then try again. If he still doesn't respond, end your session and try again later. Another major no-no is to chase him, and to punish him when he does come. Both will teach him exactly the opposite of what you are trying to accomplish.

If you are having trouble with him coming back, then you have moved too fast, and he isn't ready to proceed. Keep working on the stationing in front of you, and reinforcing him when he does come over to start a session, and then end the session with that.

Teach Skipper his name

Most of you are saying, "But he knows his name!" He probably does. But you can make it even more positive when he responds to his name.

While you are in the middle of one of your sessions, you can simply say Skipper's name, bridge and reinforce. And any time you start a session, you can follow the double blast with his name. As you progress with sessions, you can say his name and bridge when he looks up or directly responds. And that's actually why Skipper already knows his name. Up to this point, whenever you called him over, what did you do when he came? You played with him, rubbed his ears, or gave him a treat. So you trained him to recognize his name. See, you're already a trainer!

Remember that any time you use his name, and he responds to it, reinforce him, not necessarily with food (primary), but with those secondary reinforcers (play, pat on the head, scratching the ears, or a favorite toy).

I also suggest that if you are going to reprimand him, don't do it right after you call him and he comes over. Why? Because that would be reprimanding him for responding to your calling him. That would teach him to NOT come over!

You also should not use his name when scolding him ("bad dog, Skipper, bad dog"). This will teach Skipper that his name could be associated with an aversive stimulus. After all, what does Skipper really hear? Probably something like "Blah, blah, Skipper, blah, blah." He doesn't speak English but he does understand whatever stimulus follows that phrase with his name in it.

Reprimanding, scolding and other punishments are usually no good anyway, because it is simply too late. The behavior is done already, and Skipper's little brain is on to other things *(like when does he gets to run some more or pondering why he can't eat every twenty minutes)*.

Chapter 7: Let's start some training

Are we tired with working with just dogs? OK, this works great with horses and cats too (as well as any pet or animal that you may have the good luck to be hanging out with). So why don't I introduce a horse, Tex, two cats, Alger and Cheetah, and let's give Skipper a break occasionally by also working with another dog, Laddie.

Let's teach the animal to target. A "**target**" is the quintessential training tool. With a target, I have trained dolphins to do spinning jumps, tigers to stand on a scale to be weighed, whales to give me their tail so I could take a blood sample, and much, much more.

With a target, you can teach just about anything. But think in basics. How do you teach Laddie to go from point A to point B? How do you teach him to sit, or sit and stay? How do you teach a horse to go into a horse trailer?

You can do all of this with a target. You just teach them a focal point or a spot (**target**) that they go to whenever you ask. The easiest target (and cheapest) is simply your flat hand.

So armed *(no pun intended)* with your very technical and expensive training tool, you can teach a target.

Training a "target"

<u>Option 1</u>

Hold out your hand and say "target." Stare right back at Laddie while he stares at you with his head in that cute sideways look that means "huh?"

Actually, lots of people think this is how you start training…with a wing and a prayer. But it isn't. You want to make everything crystal clear to any animal you are working with. Remember, Laddie can't understand those things you call words, so you need to teach him, step by step, what the heck you are talking about.

Option 2

Teach him what a target is. Touch your hand to Laddie's nose, bridge, and then reinforce. Got that? You touch your hand to his nose, and as your "target" (hand) touches his nose, blow the whistle (**bridge**), and then give him his piece of hot dog (**reinforcer**).

Remember to take away your hand once you have blown the whistle. Do this over and over again, for two or three sessions. Then, after one of these "touch his nose" things, after you have reinforced, offer your hand again, but this time hold it about an inch away from him.

At this point, Laddie is hopefully thinking, "Hmm, Socrates has stated that if I touch this hand puteth in front of my noble nose, I will thus be rewarded in a princely fashion by hearing a dulcet tone followed by a fine chunk of preserved porcine."

OK, maybe it sounds more like "hand = whistle = yummy." Either way, I'll lay 10-1 odds he sticks his nose straight onto your hand. Bridge him (blow the whistle) when his nose hits your hand, reinforce (give him a piece of hot dog) and try again with your hand about two inches away. *(Are you picking up on a trend here?)* Baby steps, baby steps - - never rush training.

Soon you should be able to present that target (your hand) anywhere and Laddie will come over. Now you need to introduce a cue (S^d) to tell him when he should look for that target. For sea lions, tigers, and other animals, which can listen for verbal cues (as can Laddie and Skipper), you can use the word "target."

So, right before each time you present your hand, you say "target." Now you have an S^d. You say "target," Laddie looks for your hand, and goes to it.

You can also use a ball on a stick (the classic marine mammal tool).

Using a target pole can cut down on a simple problem of using the same hand for a target that you use to reinforce. When your hand is covered with hot dog juice, Laddie may start to lose his focus. So, if you want to set him up to succeed, use a different hand than your "reinforcing hand," or use a target pole.

Okay, time for another reminder on timing. What you bridge is what you get - ***not what <u>you think</u> you are bridging, but what the animal is actually doing***. I can't emphasize this enough *(which is why I keep saying it over and over again!).*

And I'm saying it again *(and not for the last time!).* Punishing a dog when it doesn't come over right away is a great example. Think about what you are punishing. Laddie doesn't know you are mad he didn't come back right away, all he knows is that when he DID come, you punished him. You are telling him "BAD" for coming over.

Using the bridge with poor timing tells the animal "good," but for the wrong thing. If I ask a beluga whale to hold its tail in my lap for a blood sample, and then bridge him at the end of the behavior as he pulls away, I am bridging a second too late.

I think I'm bridging a nice calm tail "present." If you ask me, that's probably what I'd say, **but I really bridged the whale pulling its tail AWAY.** And that was simply because of an instant in time, where I missed with the bridge. Trust me, you don't want to teach a 1600-lb whale to pull its tail away while you are holding it!

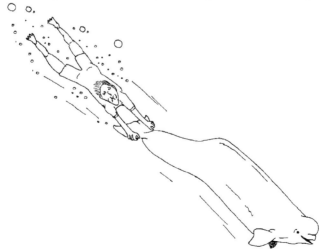

Another good example is teaching Laddie to sit, and he sits. Then you bridge him as he jumps up to get his hot dog piece. Did you bridge him for sitting? Well, you think you did. ***Actually you bridged him for jumping back up,*** and hence, the famous bouncing dog behavior. Remember - TIMING, TIMING, TIMING!

Okay, with targeting added to your behavioral repertoire, you've got the basics down. If you can answer these questions, you're ready to move on.

1. What's a bridge?
2. What's a reinforcer?
3. What's an $S^{d?}$
4. What is critical when using your bridge?

If you answered all of these correctly, we're ready to move on. So check your answers. If you didn't answer them, or you are doubtful about something, do a quick check back over the last few chapters until you're comfortable with the basic concepts. *(If you do read back, you can skip reading the autobiography a second time. It doesn't get any more exciting with more reading.)*

And your answers are:

1. A way to say good job. *(In our case, a whistle.)*
2. A reward or treat for doing the good job. *(In our case, we will use primaries, or food. Specifically, you could have just said "a hot dog piece."*
3. Something that tells Laddie what we are asking for. It is a selective cue.

4. TIMING. *(I really hope you got this right.)*

Work on the basics quite a bit. If you manage to do three sessions a day with Cheetah, or Laddie, you want to focus about 50% of each session on the basics, keeping it fresh with your animals.

So, what do you want to train first? Remember, there really are no limitations, except physical ones. *(Again, don't try to train Cheetah to dive 40 feet down in a pool to pick up different density objects. It won't work.)*

How about starting your animal training education with a great animal behavior that has lots of possible mistakes along the way? Let's teach Laddie a simple retrieval (dolphin trainer talk for "fetch"). Oops, wait a sec. Put down that Frisbee and hold on, you're not ready to go yet. Let's think about this first.

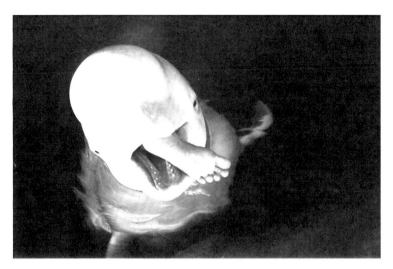

"What the...? I didn't ask you to retrieve that!"

Chapter 8: Retrievals

Any time you start training a new behavior, think about what the essence of the behavior is, no matter what you're working on. I don't mean you need to ponder the existential meaning of the behavior, just try to boil the behavior down to its simplest form.

So if you want to teach retrieval, what really is the behavior? Most people will say, "The dog getting the Frisbee." Well, let's think about it for a second. What if Laddie goes and gets the Frisbee? What does he do with it then? Think! What is actually the "final product"? What do you expect from the behavior? Want some help?

OK, if you said, "Giving me the Frisbee," give yourself a big pat on the back, or whatever reinforcer you prefer. *(A very cold ale does just fine for me.)*

Giving you the Frisbee is the entire behavior. Of course, the dog has to go get it, or chase it, or find it, but if you teach Laddie to give it to you (no matter where it is), then you are done! And you won't end up running after him, yelling "fetch" over and over again, while he happily trots away from you with a Frisbee in his mouth. So let's give it a try, shall we?

Step 1

Option 1

Throw the Frisbee and wait for Skipper to run after it. This is actually the most commonly used starting point for teaching a fetch or retrieval. It seldom works!

I know people who will insist their dogs get it right away, but those dogs are always instinctive "fetchers," such as an Australian shepherd. And does that dog wait for you to throw it? Does it come back right away? Does it play tug-of-war at the end?

You are hoping Laddie goes for it, but you don't know, and if he likes to play, he may go for it, but good luck getting it back.

Option 2

Teach Laddie to give you the Frisbee.

Think of training the behavior backwards. The last thing in the sequence of events you want Laddie to do is hand you the Frisbee. Right? So put the Frisbee in Laddie's mouth. Then, at the same time your hand is holding the Frisbee and Laddie holds the Frisbee in his mouth, bridge (whistle) and reinforce (hot dog piece).

What you want to get him to do is to actually drop it into your hand. Put the Frisbee in his mouth and as you take it back out, bridge and reinforce. At the **EXACT** same time you are doing this, you can introduce your S^d (cue). You can use "give" or "fetch" or "blue"— it doesn't matter. But right after you put the Frisbee in his mouth and right before you take it back, give him the S^d.

So here's the sequence:

a. Frisbee in mouth
b. Say "give"
c. Take the Frisbee back and as he releases, then bridge and reinforce

Ok, now he's giving you the Frisbee on command. Don't overwork it and ALWAYS reinforce with the primary. Do this in several sessions before moving on to Step 2. Actually, if Laddie seems to get it right away, you can move more quickly, but be careful to be sure he "has it."

He shouldn't drop it without the S^d, and he shouldn't play tug of war at all. If he consistently gives it to you, say seven or eight times in a row without a mistake, you are probably ready to move on.

Step 2

Option 1

Throw the Frisbee as far as you can. Look at Laddie and yell "Give!" Well, Laddie will probably be thinking, "I would give it to you, but where the heck is it, you moron?!" You have moved too quickly - - take baby steps, baby steps.

Option 2

Teach him to pick up the Frisbee. Up to this point, you have been handing it to him, so don't assume he'll make the leap from you sticking the Frisbee in his mouth to him picking it up. Work on grass or some "non-Frisbee-sliding surface" and turn the Frisbee upside down. This is another good example of setting up the animal to succeed.

If you put the Frisbee right side up on a deck, he's going to have a heck of a time picking it up, whether he knows the behavior or not. Again, the last thing you want to do in training is make the behavior more difficult than it needs to be. So set the Frisbee upside down to make it easy to pick up.

Put it right in front of him and follow this sequence:

a. Give him the S^d (say "give")
b. Wait for him to pick it up and give it to you
c. When he does, bridge and reinforce with two or three reinforcers. This is called "differential reinforcement." Some trainers call it jackpotting. It's like saying "Wow…really, really good!"

OK, I know this sounds like a leap of faith, but after lots of practice with Step 1, there is a very good chance Laddie will see the Frisbee right there, and pick it up, SO THAT HE CAN GIVE IT TO YOU AND GET BRIDGED!

Get the idea? By teaching him the one simple behavior of giving it to you, you are training him to find it and give it to you. But again, don't rush.

Step 3

At this point, you know not to wing the Frisbee 40 feet, so simply approximate the distance away from you.

a. Toss the Frisbee one foot away and say "give" as you toss (don't worry about Laddie going to get the Frisbee before you ask him. We'll fix that later)
b. After he gets it a few times in a row, try tossing it two feet away…
c. And so on, and so on

If at any point, he can't find it, or doesn't go get it, take a step back (or "regress") in your training. This is perfectly normal and may happen often in training. If Laddie blows off looking for the Frisbee at ten feet, throw it seven feet until he gets it right several times, then go back to ten. Pretty soon you should be at whatever distance you want.

Trouble-shooting up to this point

A few things could happen here:

1. Laddie may just look down at the Frisbee in Step 2 and not make an attempt to pick it up. If so, you can always help him out. Pick it up a little bit and say "give" again, and see if his natural instinct is to grab it, at which point he will give it to you.

2. You may notice the emergence of a new behavior you were *not* trying to train. This is called "superstitious behavior" and is caused by bad timing.

   Be careful with your bridge. What are we bridging? What is the behavior? To GIVE you the Frisbee. So DO NOT bridge when he grabs it out in the field or park or wherever. By doing that you are saying "good job" for running out there and grabbing it, and NOT for giving it to you. This is how you end up with a dog running around with a Frisbee in his mouth.

3. Laddie stops paying attention to you, or doesn't take the $S^{d,}$ or wanders away to sniff another dog's nether regions. This is a key indicator that the session has gone too long, and is no longer positive. Don't let your own competitive drive affect Laddie. He doesn't care if you finish the behavior in one session. He's just having a good time working, so end on a positive (like if he just went from seven feet to ten feet). STOP, and do another session later. *(Ten 8-minute sessions work much better than five 16-minute sessions)*.

Step 4

Option 1

You want Laddie to wait until you actually ASK him to go get something and give it to you. So grab his collar, and throw the Frisbee. *(Well, when you wake up covered with abrasions, maybe you want to try something else. Again, holding an animal, or pushing its body around, or "helping" them physically, does not teach them anything.)*

Option 2

We "fade" in the S^d (cue). Laddie already has heard the S^d every time you throw, drop, toss or hand him the Frisbee. There's a good chance he knows what it is for, but he has not yet been taught to **WAIT** until he hears you say it. So far you have taught him to run like the dickens any time you throw that funny round thing.

Now you want to teach him to wait. This can be a bit tricky, but it is done with your **target**, and with your **bridge**, using "selective bridging." That just means you use your bridge to tell him "THAT'S IT!" exactly when he DOESN'T go get the Frisbee after you throw it. OK, here we go.

Your target behavior should be very strong, so have Laddie target next to you, and while he is on target (touching your hand), drop the Frisbee in front of you. If he, even for an instant, stays without grabbing it, BRIDGE, reinforce quickly and then give him your retrieval S^d before he takes off on his own. *(This stuff is very tough to describe on paper. Use your gut!)*

Bridge and reinforce the "give," and then start approximating how long he waits until he hears the S^d. You are basically teaching him to actually listen for specific signals, like "target" meaning hold his nose against your palm, and "give," meaning go for the Frisbee.

Now it might seem hard to keep a dog from zipping away to get a Frisbee when you throw it, but I guarantee a Pacific white-sided dolphin moves faster… like 25 to 30 miles per hour through the water…and we taught them to wait several minutes, even through several other behaviors, before sending them to retrieve. Actually, we taught them to search the habitat whether we had just thrown something in or not, and that was a blast for them.

Teaching Laddie to search without you determining the object may not be the best idea. Who knows what he'll find out there, and whatever a dog does find, I'm not sure you'll want it. That would be like teaching a cat to retrieve whatever it searches for and finds in your back yard. In essence, you would teach them to kill birds, chipmunks, etc., just so they can do the retrieval behavior.

What's fun to retrieve for a dog or cat may not be a whole lot of fun for you, so pick and teach your object. And, yes, you can teach a cat to "fetch."

OK, so let's recap. Our hope was to train Laddie to sit next to you while you throw a Frisbee, then tell him "give" or whatever your S^d is, and then he runs out for the Frisbee, picks it up, brings it back to you, and you bridge (whistle) and reinforce (hot dog), as he gives it to you. That seems like a lot of things to teach Laddie, but all we really did was teach him to give you the Frisbee!

Want to try something else? You can certainly stop here, and train your version of Laddie for a while. The book will still be here when you get back. (And if it isn't, you can always buy a new one!)

"Buy another book? Forget it!"

Chapter 9: Training a cat?

OK, many people will tell you, "Oh, you can't train cats at all!" I've heard "they are too smart" (code for "I don't know how to train") or "they have a mind of their own." *(I certainly hope so. Again, code for poor training.)* Well, when I went to Ocean Journey, I was told we had to train tigers a certain way. I certainly wouldn't be able to train them my "dolphin" way. At least, that is what many people said.

I paid about as much attention to that as I do to child-rearing advice from 25-year-olds in the supermarket, and I went ahead and created a training program for these rather large kittens. So don't you think that if I can use these methods to train really big kittycats, about 275 pounds each, that you could do it with your normal-sized friend at home? Sure you can!

You can train Cheetah (our cat for this book) just as you trained Skipper or Laddie, and just as I have trained whales and dolphins. Start with the same basics we used on Skipper until you feel you are ready to use them in training a certain behavior. And the next step? Just pick a behavior.

What do you want to teach your cat to do? How about a cooperative behavior, since cats are reputed to be especially un-cooperative, like training Cheetah to let us clip his claws?

What's our first step? Simplify! What are we actually trying to train? Boil it down to "What is the simple behavior you are looking for?" (Think about it and come up with something BEFORE you turn the page…no cheating!)

I want to train Cheetah to _____

_____

So what did you come up with? If your answer was "have him let us clip his claws," you are thinking a little too broadly. If your answer was "have him offer us his paw"…you got it! It's really very simple. Train Cheetah to offer you his paw, and the rest is easy. Let's get started.

Step 1

Option 1

Pick up his paw and bridge. This is pretty common (and incorrect), and is also incorrect when training a dog to do a handshake. The difficulty is you are "molding" the behavior, not training it. You want it to be Cheetah's idea to hold up his paw.

Option 2

Teach Cheetah a target. And then target his paw into your hand, just like we have trained really big whales to simply roll over and lay their huge tail flukes in our laps.

Now you have already trained targeting, so getting started should be pretty easy. Simply touch Cheetah's front paw with the flat of your hand and bridge. *(OK, from now on, whenever I say "bridge," it also means to follow immediately with a reinforcer).*

At the same time you are teaching this "paw target" you can also pair your S^d with it. For example, touch or target his paw and say "PAW" at the same time, then bridge (while you still have contact).

Do this several times, and then put your hand an inch above his paw, give the $S^{d,}$ and wait. If you have done enough of the touching thing, he should target his paw right to your hand. Bridge the touch (remember your TIMING). Don't bridge right after he brings his paw to your hand, bridge at exactly the moment he "targets" his paw to the target (your hand).

You can also use a target pole to train this, but you'll have to transfer the behavior to your hand eventually anyway (so that you can hold the paw while you clip), so you may as well start out with a hand target and save yourself a step. I've said it before, I'll be saying it again — don't make the behavior harder than it has to be. Make it simple for you and Cheetah.

Step 2

Option 1

Once Cheetah is handing you his paw, grab hold of it firmly and quickly try to clip his claws. *(Then find some hydrogen peroxide and bandages for yourself, see if you can find Cheetah, and then you'll need to start the target training from scratch).* Actually, while this is meant to be a humorous option, it contains a serious message. Do not betray the training relationship and trust you have built. You'll have a heck of a time re-building it.

<u>Option 2</u>

Slowly approximate (little steps) your hand target further up and away, so that when you give the S^d ("paw"), Cheetah lifts his paw up high enough for you to work with. At the same time, slowly shift (or fade) your hand target upside down, so that he actually sets his paw in your open hand.

Again, make sure that setting his paw in your hand is something he does. Don't grab his paw or rush to that point. OK, so now Cheetah is lifting his paw up and setting it in your hand. What next?

Step 3

Now start lengthening how long he holds his paw in your hand before you bridge. This is called "extending" the behavior. In this case, it would be an "extended target" (paw to hand). Vary your times. Don't keep going longer and longer without also going back to short times and bridging.

So you want to approximate (again...taking small steps) from a ½-second in your hand to several seconds, and eventually varying the times. Your goal is for Cheetah to hold that paw in your hand until you bridge. Once Cheetah is holding that paw for a few seconds consistently, you are ready for the next step.

Step 4

Option 1

Now that he is holding his paw calmly in your hand, clip each claw.

NO! You would be moving too fast. Don't rush it. Just because Cheetah has figured out your paw target, the "paw present" behavior does **not** mean he will be fine for the introduction of a variable such as the clippers. After all, the clippers have probably been associated with restraint, discomfort, and even "quicking" his claw, causing bleeding. You need to continue to move in little steps or approximations.

Option 2

Slowly introduce Cheetah to having his paw touched with your other hand, or another object, while he stays in a calm "paw present." Here's a very good example of why I prefer a whistle bridge to a clicker. You can use both hands. While Cheetah is in "paw present," touch his paw with your other hand, and bridge. Remember, you are bridging the entire paw and touch behavior, so reinforce, and start all over with the "paw" S^d.

Each time you do a "paw present," approximate the manipulation of the paw, bridging and reinforcing each little step. *(Don't forget, this could take several sessions… don't try to do it all at once.)* Do this for several sessions, and make sure it's involved in at least one session a day.

Eventually push the claws out for differing amounts of time, bridging each time. After a few sessions, you should be able to actually manipulate each claw and press on his pad to expose the claw, all with Cheetah calmly waiting for the bridge. By now, Cheetah will let you do almost anything with that paw.

Two quick notes:

1. Once you train this with one paw, it will be very simple to "transfer" to the others. In other words, you won't have to train it all over again for the other paws, although you will have to train a roll-over so that Cheetah can offer his back paws without falling on his face *(which is kinda funny, but a tad counter-productive)*.

2. Remember again to keep your sessions short and positive, especially with cats, as their focus isn't quite as strong as dogs *(or, before cat people show up with protest banners outside my house, their attention span doesn't hold as long in a training session)*. This is just a general tendency, and is part of knowing your animal's characteristics. Your cat may do 20-minute sessions just fine. Mine doesn't.

Step 5

Introduce the clippers. Simply show them to Cheetah while you are holding his paw, and bridge. Then touch his paw with them and bridge, and continue to get him comfortable with the presence of these nice scissor things. *[Remember these little steps called approximations]*

Once he seems very comfortable with them being around his paws, on his paw or even around a claw, snip just past the very tip. In other words, don't actually clip any of the claw. If he stays calm, bridge.

A big reminder here! If he startles, pulls his claw back, or tries to, do not hold on to his paw. Wait, don't bridge or reinforce, take a few steps back *(regress)*, bridging just for acceptance of the clippers, or even just for a calm "paw" behavior, and judge whether you want to try again in that session.

You only want to bridge if he stays completely calm and doesn't pull, or tug, or yowl.

If he does stay completely calm, bridge and reinforce him for the behavior of staying calm with the clippers snipping. After a few times of this, try clipping just the very tip of his claw, again bridging him, if he stays calm. Now you are almost there, and it's just a matter of approximating a bit more claw each time you work the behavior.

But remember, you taught Cheetah a game, and that game is the "paw" behavior. You should play the game very often, but only actually clip his nails once a month or so after the behavior is trained.

With whales, we trained them to give us their tails and then hold them in our laps for two, three or four minutes. We taught them to allow us to poke and wiggle their tails, and play games with pushing them up and down in the water. We also practiced taking blood every day, making it into one of those games, BUT we only actually inserted a needle in their tail for a sample once a month. You want to do the same with any "cooperative behaviors" you teach your critters.

I have trained the exact same claw clipping behavior with harbor seals *(yep, they have claws on their flippers)*, sea otters, and I've thought about trying it on tigers, so your Cheetah shouldn't faze you.

Recap time again. You trained a very simple behavior, right? All you are really doing is asking Cheetah for his paw, and then extending how long he keeps it there and how much you can fiddle with it. Simple.

What else do you think we could train with these exact steps? How about "shake" with Skipper's paw? Or, as we did with Cheetah, can we train Skipper to offer each paw so we can clean the mud off each one when he comes into the house? These steps will also let you teach horses to hold up each hoof for cleaning and trimming, without having a 2000-pound horse lean on you.

So every time you look at training a behavior with one animal, consider how the exact same approach will work on any other animal, which is the whole idea of "Whales with Fur."

Having fun yet? I am, so why don't we move on to another behavior, and another animal. Let's work with Tex, our horse. Again, many will say horses are different, and that they can't be trained this way. To which I say "balderdash"! *(Cool word, huh? I put it right up there with "dad-gummit.")*

Granted, traditional horse training is not the same *(although much of it is a type of operant conditioning...do you know which type?)*, but that doesn't mean that treating them like whales with fur (hair in this case) won't work. In fact, it works very well.

Chapter 10: A horse is a horse, of course...

So now we need a behavior for Tex. We have learned how to train him to retrieve (and yes, it will work) and how to lift each hoof for manipulation, trimming, etc. What else will help us out?

My tendency is to always think of behaviors that are not only fun, but also are very useful tools, so how about teaching a horse to go into its trailer? From their usual behavior, we can either assume horses don't like trailers, *or* maybe it was just never made to be a positive experience for them. The key would be to make it another one of those training games.

So, first make sure you've got Tex working with all the basics, just as we did with Skipper and Cheetah. And then what do you do? Boil it down. What is the simple behavior you are looking for?

Does Tex need to understand he's going for a ride? Do you need to teach him several complex behaviors? Take a few minutes to think about your desired behavior while I answer the "what kind of operant conditioning" trivia question.

Did you figure out what kind of operant conditioning is prevalent in riding? A great deal of horse training is negative reinforcement. When someone is riding English, they pull the reins in the direction they want to go, which puts pressure on the horse's mouth. The horse goes that direction, which relieves the pulling, so something was subtracted (the pressure of the reins), which increased the likelihood of the behavior.

The horse turns to remove the tugging, and removing the tugging is reinforcing. The same is true with leg pressure and spurs. Some would say spurs are punishment, but it depends on intent. If you use the spurs properly, the horse quickens its pace and the spur is removed. That's negative reinforcement and effective training.

If you use the spurs because your horse won't go fast enough and you're mad and just "spurring" the horse, it seems the same, but that isn't effective communication of what you want. It's just taking out your frustration with spurs. Although this is a form of punishment, it isn't the "training kind of punishment," as you really are not decreasing any behavior. You're just mad or frustrated.

The horse isn't "out to get you." It's learned it can get away with plodding along.

Okay, let's go train a horse! Did you think about what you have to train? By now, you are probably thinking, "Heck, this isn't complicated. We just need to teach Tex to target!"

Good job! *(Give yourself a treat.)* You are well on your way to training, not only your dog or cat, but your horse, as well (or anything else you want to train).

The simple behavior is to teach Tex to go to a target. The difference from our other targeting behavior is that <u>YOU won't be with the target</u>. But it is still just teaching targeting.

Basically, you want to teach Tex to go from Point A (you) to Point B (the target), and to go by himself.

Leading him into the trailer may seem easier, but then you have to get out of the trailer, and what if he doesn't want to go in? Leading him in could become painful - for you. So we will train him to go in, on S^d, from being with you to being comfortably in the trailer with the door shut behind him. You've already got it down to your basic behavior, so you are all set to begin!

Step 1

<u>Option 1</u>

Tell the horse to go into the trailer to your hand target. *(Uh-oh…your hand is with you! And you aren't in the trailer!)*

<u>Option 2</u>

"Desensitize" Tex to the new variable, the target pole. Don't assume something new in your hand will be automatically accepted. Teach the animal to get comfortable with any new training tool, just like we did with Skipper and the Frisbee or Cheetah and the clippers. And you don't need to use your hand as a target, that's just a very convenient one. For Tex, let's train his target behavior to a **target pole**.

For a horse, I would use a ½-length broom handle, with a softball at the end (just drill a hole in the softball and attach it to your "target" pole). And now you possess another high-tech, state-of-the-art training tool.

Now train targeting just like you did with your other animals. First, introduce the pole during training sessions. *(By the way, just as with Cheetah and Tex, don't forget about building that training relationship, and teaching a bridge, etc.)*

Also, baby carrots work pretty well as reinforcers for horses. Watch your hip pouch though, a horse can reach it! You don't want Tex reinforcing himself during the training session! Try sliding it around behind your back.

Don't use the pole right away, just have it with you so the horse gets used to its presence. Once he seems comfortable, move to Step 2.

And by the way, all the animals are male in this book because all the real life critters they are based on happen to be male. Neither gender is easier or harder to train, and I certainly have no preference. So again, before anyone

Whales with Fur

shows up to picket outside my house, Skipper, Cheetah, Tex, and Alger (the sea lion) just happen to be males.

Where was I? Oh, yeah, once Tex seems comfortable with the target pole, move to Step 2.

Step 2

<u>Option 1</u>

Make those "kissie" noises like people do when they want an animal to come over, and wait for the horse to move. *(A good book or a Snickers bar is recommended in this option, 'cuz you will be waiting for a long while).*

<u>Option 2</u>

Train Tex to target and follow the target pole. How did we train targeting?

Touch the target (softball at the end of the pole) gently to Tex's nose and bridge. Do this several times and then hold the target an inch or two away. See if he comes over (or in the case of an inch, moves his head fractionally) so he can touch the target. Bridge, and keep approximating him to look for and touch that target.

At the same time you are doing this, make sure to pair a "target" S^d with the training, as you will need it in a bit. By the way, just presenting the target pole is an S^d. You are asking for a behavior simply by presenting the target.

When you are asking for a remote target, however, you will need a verbal S^d like the word "target." Pair the word with the presentation of the target pole.

Soon Tex will begin following you and your softball wherever you go.

Step 3

<u>Option 1</u>

Use an apple instead of a softball for your target because the horse will definitely go to it. *(Your horse will certainly stay on the target until it's gone. Of course, then you need a new target AND Tex just reinforced himself for eating the target pole!)*

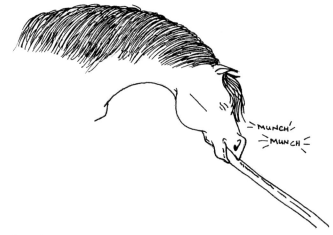

<u>Option 2</u>

Train Tex to go to the target away from you. Once Tex is consistently targeting, set the pole in the ground upright, about two feet away from you. Introduce a visual S^d, like the sweep of your arm, ending with pointing at the target, and give the verbal S^d.

Now you are no longer holding the pole. When Tex walks a step and touches the target, bridge and reinforce. If, on the other hand, he stares at you, thinking, "What target, you silly biped?" you can start with it closer, or even in front of him, as long as you don't hold it. As he gets consistent with going to the target (and away from you), keep increasing the distance.

Now we have a tricky dilemma with reinforcing. There are two ways to do that. Don't forget that when you bridge, you are saying "good job," and here's your reinforcer (carrot). Well, that means Tex walks back over to you to get it.

Since we are training him specifically to go to a spot and stay there, you can walk with him, and bridge and reinforce when you both get there. *(A better way is to train an "A to B" with two trainers…we'll talk about that in a minute.)*

Once Tex takes your pointing and verbal "target" S^ds, and goes to wherever you put the target, then you are ready to work with extending the target, getting him to stay on it longer, just as we did with Cheetah's paw present.

Step 4

Option 1

You are done. Take his lead rope and pull him into the trailer. *(Remember the bandages, hydrogen peroxide, and general pain related to some of the other Option 1's? Never rush a behavior!)*

Option 2

Using both regular and remote targeting, you can start working on an "extended target." *(In fact, it might work better to start on this before you work on the remote target)*. Simply wait a teeny bit longer before you bridge and, if Tex stays on the target for that longer time, then you are on your way. Don't be discouraged if he doesn't stay on it at first *(I would be surprised if he did)*, because you haven't taught him to, yet. He will probably touch the target and then swing his head to you for his carrot. Make sure not to give him one, and ask again.

Remember, taking baby steps (small approximations) is the key, or you won't catch that extra millisecond he stays on the target. But with patience, you'll have him holding on that target until he hears his bridge.

Once he is consistently staying on target, at any location, we are ready to introduce the trailer.

Step 5

Desensitize Tex to the new variable, which at this point is the trailer.

Bring Tex near the trailer. Plant your target in the ground next to the trailer door and give your S^d. After he goes to the target a few times, try positioning it just inside the trailer door. (Figure out a way to affix the target easily to different points in the trailer. Your best bet is to be able to simply wedge the handle into the sides.)

Again, give him the S^d and work the behavior further and further into the trailer, always making it very positive to be in the trailer. At this point, stay with Tex so that you can reinforce him as he reaches that target.

Once you have worked him all the way to the front of the trailer (remember, small steps, and don't be afraid to regress back a step or two…and end on success!), find a good spot to mount your target. You could also attach a softball to the front wall of the trailer, and make a permanent target. You want Tex to take your "target" S^d from you standing outside the trailer, and go into that target at the very front (by the cab). Once he targets there, bridge, go in and reinforce.

Extend his time on the target so that you can walk in after him, and bridge and reinforce after he stays for a few seconds. Now the hard part is closing the door, since you want him on target until the door closes, but then you're going to have a tough time bridging and reinforcing from behind the door.

Step 6a

Once Tex is very comfortable moseying in to target, give him the S^d (verbal and visual), and while he goes to the target, you can move around to reinforce him from the cab (if you have access from the cab to the trailer). This way, you can bridge him and reinforce him for staying in the trailer, while you are outside the trailer.

You can also use the "old toss method" (throwing the reinforcement to an animal who is at a remote station) if you have no way to reinforce from outside, but make sure you have good aim, and that Tex knows its coming! If you happen to whack him on his nether regions with a carrot AND you are standing behind him…well, you might train "hoof to trainer targets" without even trying.

We used the toss reinforcer with whales during water work, where a beluga was 20-30 feet away in the pool where it would do its behaviors, and we would bridge and toss the reinforcer. (*Again, good aim was important, and more than one herring ending up plonkin' the whales on the head…it doesn't hurt, but it might diminish the reinforcing qualities of the fish*).

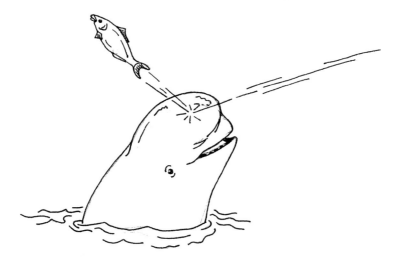

You might be wondering why all of a sudden we have a Step 6a. Well, like all training, there are often options, and that's what we'll talk about as an alternative to 6a, in (*you guessed it*) 6b.

Step 6b

Train a secondary reinforcer. Look back at the "lingo" on page 20. A conditioned, or secondary, reinforcer is something we teach Tex is positive, like when you scratch Skipper's ears, or give Tex a nice pat on the neck. It is <u>not</u> a food reinforcer.

How will this help us in this case? Well, if you can't find a way to bridge and deliver a primary reinforcer once the door is closed (which, remember, we have not done yet) how about a **verbal reinforcer**? We can train Tex with a secondary reinforcer that can be used once the door is closed.

Training a secondary is quite simple. In fact, you already have a very effective one. Do you know what it is? The whistle!

Every time Tex hears the whistle, he gets a primary reinforcer after it. So that whistle has become a very powerful reinforcer all on its own, even if you don't always follow with a primary.

But let me emphasize that if you abuse the use of a secondary, that is, you don't often also reinforce the secondary with a primary, then you run the risk of having it "extinguished" and no longer positive. In fact, it might become a source of frustration for Tex, Skipper or Cheetah.

Don't forget the trust element in training! For ease in understanding the concept, let's train another secondary AFTER the bridge to use in this case. The word "good" is effective, and you can use it while riding, jumping or eventing with Tex.

So to train the secondary, during your sessions with Tex (which shouldn't only be trailer work anyway), begin saying "good" after you bridge, but before you give the primary. Also work it as a behavior. Say "good," then bridge and reinforce. Both of these methods will teach Tex that the word "good" is a positive thing, and by pairing it with your primary or food reinforcer, you create a secondary, or non-food reinforcer.

Once you have done that over and over and over again, you have a secondary reinforcer. This can be a very effective tool, should you find yourself training, and lacking primaries (carrots). If you are riding in a cross-country event, and Tex makes a great jump, and you want to reinforce *(which is very difficult with a carrot in mid-jump)* you can simply say a crisp "good" at the very pinnacle of the behavior. Tex's jumps will get higher and better using this secondary.

Okay, once you feel the "good" is a strong secondary reinforcer, you are ready to work with the door.

So now you have Tex doing an extended target all the way into the trailer for several seconds. Once you have him calm and waiting for that bridge, let's move on.

Step 7

Option 1

Slam the door shut quickly before Tex can get out. *(This will work…once, and then you should be ready to start the training all over again, with a handicap in the trust area.)*

Option 2

Desensitize Tex to your changing position, and to the moving door.

Now, while Tex is targeting inside the trailer, you should teach him not to worry about you moving around inside and outside the trailer. So leave where you are reinforcing from, take a step back, and if he stays calm, bridge and reinforce. You are teaching him to stay on that target, whether you leave the trailer, no matter where you are.

Slowly approximate yourself away from the front and inside the trailer towards the back, but don't forget to bridge with each further step, and then go back to reinforce your bridge. Once Tex doesn't care where you are wandering to, start working with the door.

Slowly approximate him to stay at station while you, with your hand on the door, make a small movement of the door, then a larger movement, working in small steps all the way up to actually shutting the door.

If he stays calm and on target, bridge, swing the door right back open, and rush over to reinforce with multiple carrots. You swing the door back open because, just like all of our steps, you want to slowly approximate how long the door stays closed. Remember you've built a trust with Tex and you don't want to have that door mess up that relationship by shutting him in too early. Also remember to use your secondary ("good") often before giving the primary. (You will want to vary this by not always using the secondary.)

So now Tex will go straight into the trailer, target near the front, wait while you shut the door, and find it all a rather fun and rewarding game. But you are still re-opening the door, going in and reinforcing with a primary. So now all that diligent work at introducing the word "good" comes through.

Step 8

Train Tex to stay put while the door closes, and make it positive after the door stays shut.

The hard part, as we discussed earlier, is how to bridge and reinforce with the door shut. If you have access to the horse area from the cab, you could run around, climb in, bridge and reinforce from the cab. But you can also close the door, bridge if he stays on target, and say "good" as a reinforcer. Your whistle is positive and your secondary is positive. So Tex has been told "good job" and received his reinforcer, and the door stays shut, and he is in the trailer! And he thinks it's a game!

Remember to play the game often without taking Tex to whatever location you want to trailer him to. Speaking of which, how do we now teach him that riding in the trailer is fun?

Step 9

Approximate driving distances, making each small step positive. Sounds familiar, doesn't it? This works exactly the same for taking Skipper, Laddie, Alger or Cheetah to the vet.

Once you are done with training through Step 8, start with very small driving distances while you bridge and reinforce Tex for staying calm while the trailer moves, even if you only drive five feet.

Make this part of your training game. So a session one day might be going into the trailer, having the door shut, then opened, then other behaviors, like lifting hooves on S^d.

The next session would be going into the trailer, the door being shut, and then going for a quick drive around the farm. The third session Tex doesn't work with the trailer at all, and the fourth he goes for two quick rides.

After several days and several sessions, it really doesn't matter where you are going; it's just a game for Tex.

Fun step

You can also add a second S^d that only means go into the trailer. Introduce "IN" or "TRAILER" when you are training Tex to ramble in. Once you have paired the new S^d with the targeting behavior several times, you can even pull the target and just give him the verbal "trailer" S^d, and he'll go right in.

So you would do your visual S^d (the arm sweep towards the trailer), give the verbal S^d ("trailer"), and when Tex walks in, you close the door, bridge and give your secondary ("good").

When you open the door, either at your destination or at whatever point you open it in a training session, I would reinforce him with a few carrots. (Don't bridge. What would you be bridging?).

It is also important to reinforce that secondary with your primary, so you could do a quick session of just re-training the secondary a few times. Bridge, then say "good" and follow with a carrot.

And remember, you can always reintroduce the target if he gets confused as to what you are asking for. Taking a step back, as we keep saying, is all part of training

This can certainly seem complicated when reading it, but all we really did was train more targeting! That's all this behavior is - searching for, finding, and staying on the target, with some variables (like a trailer) tossed in.

Chapter 11: Look at me…
I'm training!

Yes, you are! Let's take a look back. With all that we accomplished in the last chapter, we only used a simple target, no matter how complicated the behavior may seem. Simplify, simplify, simplify. Did I mention make it simple?

Some behaviors seem very complicated, but in reality are very simple. Some behaviors that seem very simple can be quite complicated. And the last thing you should do, as a trainer, is to overcomplicate things. I know lots of trainers who use 15 steps where four will work. Of course, they would say I use four steps where 15 are needed, which illustrates a great point. There is never only one way to train an animal.

Now you've trained Skipper, Cheetah and Tex to do quite a bit. They all station, target, offer paws or hooves *(remember, use the same ideas no matter what you are training)*, retrieve, and happily jump or walk into a vehicle for transport. And you can take what you've learned so far and train so much more.

Let's look at several "classic" behaviors, and go through the process for each one. In fact, I'll give you the behaviors and you figure out how you want to train them. Try not to read ahead. One of the purest thrills in learning to train is figuring out the next step, or knowing what to do next without anyone telling you. Learning "on the job," so to speak, is one of the best ways to learn how to train, and it is the best way to hone your own training instinct.

We'll start with Skipper and Laddie, and some "dog" behaviors. *(Remember, you can teach these same behaviors to any critter!)*

Here are the behaviors:

1. Sit
2. Down
3. Stay
4. Roll over
5. Play dead
6. Get something from the fridge and bring it to you

Take your time. Use a notebook to jot down some thoughts on training each one. Actually, recording each of your steps as you train is a very good way to track your progress and trouble-shoot the behavior should you get stuck *(and all trainers get stuck)*. After you've worked out all these behaviors and how you might train them, then you can turn the page.

Okay, check your notebooks. Did you simplify or boil down what each behavior is, and what you want to train?

1. Sit

What is the behavior? OK, don't think too long; you just want Laddie to sit down on his haunches (but not lie down and not bounce back up again).

Training it? How about using that targeting thing he learned earlier? While Laddie is at station in front of you, simply lift the target (hand or target pole) above his nose and back over his head. His tendency will be to follow the target with his nose (because that's what he is supposed to touch the target with). As any dog looks up and then moves its nose backwards, it automatically sits down.

(This should look exactly like a coyote when its head is back to howl. See why they sit when their head is like that?) This works great, and you are teaching him to sit, rather than molding him by pushing his behind down for him. As soon as Laddie sits, bridge and reinforce, and then just approximate the time sitting to longer periods. Eventually, he will sit until bridged.

If you bridge a little too late, think about what you are bridging — standing back up. This leads to the famous "bouncing dog" syndrome. Many people believe their dog just "doesn't like to sit for too long," or "can't understand to keep sitting." In reality, he has been well trained to bounce like that. Be careful of those "superstitious behaviors" (ones you train accidentally). Paying attention to your TIMING will take care of that.

While training the behavior, you are teaching an S^d at the same time (your target, or hand moving backwards over his head) and you should pair a verbal S^d as well. How about something really cutting edge like "sit"?

After pairing the S^d with the hand motion and the behavior, you are ready to use just the S^ds and fade out the targeting. In other words, once Laddie is sitting when you say "sit" or give your hand S^d, he doesn't need to actually target anymore. But remember, if the behavior breaks down, you can always go back a step.

2. Down

What's the behavior you wrote down? This one is also a tad obvious. Sometimes figuring out the behavior is rather easy, so don't over-think it and make it hard.

Training it? I'm going to take a wild guess and assume you have already thought "targeting." You would be right again. Is this starting to sound too easy? I told you almost anything could be trained with a target.

So we simply ask Laddie for a target on the ground. Now you may just have him lean over to target, which is why you would slowly lead him down with a target, and he'll tend to lie down. If he is still leaning, or only puts his front paws on the ground, try pulling the target way from him as he tries to target to it on the ground. This will cause him to quite naturally rest his haunches along with his front legs.

Don't get discouraged with an excited dog that loves the sessions, and doesn't lie down or sit right away. Patience is very important. If you train it, it will come. When he doesn't get bridged (which hopefully he doesn't if he doesn't lie down), he'll start trying something else and that's when you'll get the behavior from him. Animals learn just as much from not being bridged as they do when they are bridged.

So, in your notebook, did you write "training an extended down"? Or "fading in an S^d"? You should be an old hand at that by now. Simply approximate him staying down there until you bridge, and again, as you're training this, pair your verbal S^d with your hand signal.

What's your hand signal? What's easy to fade in and already part of your training process? What were you doing with your hand target as you trained this? Moving it towards the ground? Then how about your S^d being your flat hand gong from in front of Laddie straight down to the ground? By pairing this S^d with "down," you have

Hank, the elephant seal, was really great at "sit, down, stay." Of course, he did weigh 1500 pounds!"

two S^ds! And remember, once the S^d is in place, you can fade out the actual target part.

3. Stay (Sit/Stay or Down/Stay)

Ever want to eat a nice quiet meal without a cold nose on your knee? Or, you'd like to have Laddie wait on your porch while you retrieve a poorly thrown newspaper from the yard? "Stay" is merely an extended "sit" or an extended "down." Remember how we trained an extended target? Same idea for extending a behavior like "sit" or "down." You simply teach them the behavior continues until you bridge.

Option 1

Put 'em on a short chain and connect it to a tree. They'll stay for sure

Option 2

Option 2, extending the behavior, certainly is more fun. Let's use "down" as an example. If you ask Laddie for a "sit" and then a "down," you now have a dog in the down position that will pop back up when you bridge. Up to now, you probably always bridged in less that two seconds of the behavior. I guarantee Laddie will bounce up in a normal time for the behavior whether you bridge or not. Try it out.

So now you want to extend past the original time you bridged before. What else should you do as you approximate longer intervals into the behavior? How about pairing a separate S^d with the future new behavior.

Ask for a "down," and bridge after one second, then move to one and a half seconds, then two, three, five, and so on. Right after each "down" S^d, pair the verbal S^d "hold" or "stay," then bridge for your time extended in the "down" behavior. Once you have him waiting for that bridge, you can start approximating how far you go away from him, with him staying put.

When you bridge, make sure you either toss the reinforcement to him, or walk back before you bridge so you can reinforce when you do. You do not want Laddie to jump up at the bridge and come over for his reinforcement (unless you then ask him to "come"). It is a good idea to toss reinforcers as you train distance from Laddie, then you can reinforce him for staying, and continue to train the behavior without starting over by going all the way back to Laddie.

Also, it helps in the early stages if he stays in the down position while you reinforce and move on. If you always have to ask for "sit," then "down," then "stay" each time you start, you'll be working on the behavior forever. The trick to having Laddie stay down is to make sure he doesn't have to get up just to get to you for reinforcement. When you start extending the time of a "down" behavior, bridge and reinforce right down there with him.

In a fairly short time you should have Laddie waiting for that bridge before he does anything else. You can literally extend the "down" to last quite a while. It helps to reinforce without the bridge while he is still in that long "stay."

4. Roll-over

What was the behavior you wrote down? Is rolling over the behavior? Or is it following a target in a circle? Either way, I think we're seeing a trend here.

Training it? What do you think? We could train it like I have with harbor seals. We taught them to spin in the water, and then used the same S^d on land, and we had rolling harbor seals! But harbor seals are fairly easy to teach to roll, since they're built to roll.

All that aside, I don't think we want to teach a dog to spin in the water just yet, so we'll have to use the tools at hand. And you have already trained sit and down, so you're halfway there. And for the rest, how about some targeting!? You'll need to start with "sit" and then "down."

Once Laddie is in the down position, use your hand target. (A target pole also works very well. You can make a dog-sized one with a baseball, or one of those nylaballs on a smaller pole and a target follow. Remember, don't let him reach the target, he should just follow it to guide him to do the rollover.

Slowly move your target in a circular motion from above his head off to one side, just like teaching him to sit, except he's following the target over to the side. Once you get him to follow that target half way over on to his back, you're almost home free. Just continue the target follow and he'll roll right back onto his stomach, and then BRIDGE! Don't forget to bridge as he's still rolling, as you want him to roll, not sit still. And you already are training the S^d!

The motion you are making with your target is a circular motion in front of his head. What better S^d for a rolling behavior? Just fade out the target pole over time and you'll end up simply doing a quick rolling motion with your hand. You can pair a verbal "roll" with the training as well, so you could eventually just say "roll" and off he'll go!

5. Play dead

The behavior? Isn't it just falling down and lying on his side? With a specific S^d? And didn't you just train Laddie to do a "down" and to lie on his side? Kind of like a quarter roll-over?

A fur seal "jug-handling," which looks remarkably like your dog should when playing "dead."

Training it? Now you just need him to do a "down" and then a partial "roll over." So ask for a "down," and go back to using a target to start the roll (use the target rather than a "roll" S^d so that you don't end up with Laddie playing dead when you ask for a roll).

We are putting two behaviors together to make a new one, so don't bridge following the "down," just go straight from the "down" into leading him over onto his side. And don't worry; you actually reinforced the "down" by asking for another behavior. See how training can get complicated?

Remember how powerful the timing of your whistle is? When you start to lead Laddie over like you did when we trained "roll over," use your bridge to teach him to stop when he is on his side. This is called **"selective bridging."**

Tell him "good job" when he is on his side, and that's where he'll stop. Be careful not to work this behavior and the roll too close together in a session or you will end up with a confusing combination for Laddie. Remember, he cannot read your mind. Always make it as clear as possible.

Once he smoothly takes the "down" S^d and flops over consistently following your target, you can "fade in" a new S^d, such as shooting your finger at him. Just use the target to get him to do the behavior and as he does the half-roll, pair your new verbal S^d "bang" with it. After doing this for a few sessions, you can fade out the target, and just keep the finger "gun."

So you can train all these simple and classic behaviors with a target. And it is useful for all animals. I just used Laddie and Skipper because most people associate those behaviors with dogs.

But how about teaching a horse to stretch before a ride or a lesson? How about using the target pole to have them stretch their necks out (target his head to his shoulders) or stretching out their legs by teaching them to target their hooves to the target? And how do you think horses are trained for "fall dead" behavior in westerns? Can you say "targeting"?

How about a classic "heel" behavior? Do you need a leash and a choke collar? Or how about you just teach a "target follow" with Laddie following your hand target, which happens to be at your side. Then couldn't you just fade in a verbal S^d, like "heel," and fade out your hand? *(What type of operant conditioning is in play when using a choke collar, if it is used properly?)*

With cats, you can target-train all the same behavior as dogs. Ever want to get your cat to go on a walk? Train it just like "heel" with a dog. And yes, you could teach it to play dead as well, although with my cats, I'm not sure anyone could tell the difference.

So targeting those simple behaviors is great, but what about complex behaviors. Like teaching Skipper to get a cold beer from the fridge? This is an excellent example of breaking a complex behavior down and figuring out your training steps. You have all the tools now, so figure it out while we answer the choke collar question above.

If the dog moves in the direction you want it to, the tight collar loosens, or is removed…in other words, **negative reinforcement**. By doing the wanted behavior, an aversive stimulus (tight chain) is removed (negative) and the likelihood of the behavior repeating is increased (reinforcement). So why not use a choke collar instead of a target?

Well, targeting is more fun, in my opinion, and more challenging to train, but I don't like the collars because they get misused 90% of the time. Hauling back on a choke chain does nothing but scare the daylights out of a dog. Gentle pressure works fine, but again, most folks don't use the tools correctly, and that is why I suggest not trying to use them at all. Use this whale stuff and you'll do fine!

6. Get something from the fridge and bring it to you

Break it down, and, like retrieval, go backwards. Let's say you're going to ask Skipper to get a beer from the refrigerator. What is the last thing Skipper needs to do?

Give you the beer. Hey, this sounds like retrieval! And it is! So your first step is:

Train Skipper to retrieve a beer can. Don't worry about the fridge, or anything else, just train the simple retrieval. What's next?

Retrieval from a different room. He's got to find the beer can to bring it to you. Looking in a different room is a whole new variable.

Your next step is: Approximate yourself out the door of the room you want Skipper to retrieve from.

So once you've taught him to retrieve the can, you want to start working the behavior in the kitchen. Just because you trained Skipper to retrieve the Frisbee does not mean he will automatically understand getting the can, but he'll get the idea quickly.

Work the retrieval in the kitchen, and slowly move to where you are giving him the S^d ("retrieve") from the door of the kitchen (setting up the can in front of the fridge will save some time later). Keep approximating yourself farther out the door each time you work the behavior, until you and Skipper are in the family room and he has to go get the can from the kitchen. Then we are ready for the next step.

Have you broken down the next step into a simple behavior? Right, get the can out of the fridge.

Open the fridge door, and set the can on the bottom shelf, away from other items. Set it where Skipper can easily reach it. Remember: set him up to succeed.

Leave the door open! He doesn't have that step yet.

While standing next to the open door, ask him to retrieve again. If Skipper has trouble finding the can on the fridge shelf, make it easier for him. Once he knows it's there, I guarantee his retrieval behavior will go well. Once he does find the can, start moving yourself out of the kitchen again, just as you did with training the basic retrieval.

Okay, now Skipper will take the "retrieve" S^d from the family room and go to the open fridge in the kitchen, but you probably don't want your fridge open all day. So here's what seems like the hard part — opening the fridge.

Now the next step is to Teach Skipper to open the fridge so he can get the can, which he will then bring to you.

Okay, do you know what's cool about this? Skipper knows all of this stuff, except opening the fridge. That's what is so important about breaking down and simplifying the behaviors. Otherwise, you might have started with teaching Skipper to open the fridge. But, since you approached it in a "Whales with Fur" way, you almost have everything trained!

So how do you teach him to open the fridge? Make sure he is very consistent on the retrieval part first. And make sure to set him up to succeed. *(Don't put a nice ham next to the beer can!)* Put the beer can in the fridge and partially close the door, making it very easy to push open.

Ask for the retrieval. If Skipper doesn't nudge the door and get the can, make it even easier, with the door open most of the way. Skipper will be looking for that can. Approximate him (still baby steps) to nudging that door open from an almost shut position. Work the behavior until he is very consistent and gets the can every time, no mistakes.

Now let's try that door shut all the way. It might take a while to get the idea of nudging hard enough to open the door, but that is what training is all about… patience. Once he does nudge it open and finds the can, he needs to bring it to you. When he does, you are done!

You now have a dog that will go from the family room to the kitchen and get you a beer (or a water bottle, or whatever). And all you did was train some variables (location and finding the object) on a simple retrieval! Good job!

But another point to keep in mind is that Skipper may use his trained powers for evil and open the fridge whenever he wants a snack. Hopefully not, as most animals look at training sessions as unique and don't apply them outside the session.

We taught dolphins to jump, but they never jumped over gates to other pools. But if Skipper does turn to crime, use avoidance. Put a child lock on the fridge, or don't give him access to the kitchen when you are not there, or leave only cans on the shelf he can reach. But again, I would be surprised if that happens.

So now we've covered several training basics, and you see how you can use those basics to train what used to seem like complicated behaviors.

But perhaps we've gone past what many of you are hoping to use training for, like teaching Skipper to not bark, or Laddie to not dig, or Cheetah to not destroy your furniture, or Tex not to clamp his teeth shut when you try to put in the bit.

What about all that stuff? That's where punishment comes in, right? Well, you could try punishment, but you can handle all of these behaviors with the same tools you have now, and by remembering a few of the "thoughts" about training that we talked about earlier.

Chapter 12: Dogs will be dogs; self-reinforcing behaviors

Okay, so normally it is boys will be boys, but there are lots of dog, cat and horse habits that are extremely annoying, yet we blame it on the old "that's what dogs (cats, horses, etc) do" excuse. So what? That doesn't mean they should be left to bark, dig, or scratch, or be a general pain in the neck.

The first natural tendency in all of us, in response to many unwanted behaviors, is lots of aversive stimuli. What you **think** you are doing is "positive punishment," but remember what is most important in training? **Timing**, right?

Well, did you apply your punishment at the exact moment Skipper was digging a hole? Did you yell "NO BARK" at Laddie, even though he doesn't have any idea what that means? And did you pick Cheetah up and fling him across the room after he demolished your couch, at exactly the moment he was scratching? Probably not.

Many of these behaviors happen when you are not around, because it gives them something to do, they are natural behaviors, and it seems to be a lot of fun. We call these "**self-reinforcing behaviors**." The animals do the behavior, get reinforced by doing it, and basically train themselves to keep on doing them. This is true for barking, digging, clawing furniture, and so on.

A great example of self-reinforcing behavior, and why it is very challenging to get rid of, is a bit R-rated, but a long time ago there was a young male northern fur seal, who, during a show, would …um…have relations with a white boat buoy up on the deck (which was also the stage) in front of the entire crowd. This was a very difficult habit to break, as his behavior was VERY self-reinforcing. In that case, the best bet would be to remove his opportunity by getting rid of the buoy.

This brings us to back to one of those thoughts to keep in your head - a key principle and the essence of good training:

REINFORCE DESIRED RESPONSES; AND IGNORE UNWANTED RESPONSES.

Basically, pay no attention to that doggie barking in the window. Punishment does not work anyway, unless your timing is right on. And if you do respond with an intended punishment, is it stronger than the reinforcing quality of the behavior itself?

If I had managed to give that fur seal a smack in the face at exactly the point he …ah, attempted intimacy with a buoy *(a very bad idea, by the way)*, would that be enough to decrease the behavior happening again? Or, would the behavior itself cause a more powerful tendency to increase the likelihood of the behavior?

Does whacking Skipper on the behind for digging make him stop digging or does he adjust to doing it when you're not there? (*This is a principle that absolutely terrifies me as I watch my four children grow towards teenage-hood*).

So how do we fix self-reinforcing behaviors? There are a few different approaches we could take.

1. Avoidance - Remove the opportunity

Avoidance is very effective, but has its limitations. For example, removing the fur seal's lady friend, the buoy, was avoidance. You run the risk of him taking out his "urges" on something else, but at least it won't be on stage. Hopefully.

A digging dog *(sounds like a country-western song)*: You could…

- Cement over your yard
- Never let him out of the house without a human being attached.

These will remove his opportunity to dig. Of course, now he'll chew up your house, and your yard can be leased out as a parking lot.

The clawing cat *(sounds like a nouveau tea shop)*:

> • Remove all the carpets and furniture in the house
> • Have Cheetah de-clawed (Some folks don't like this one. I'm not promoting or discouraging it…it is simply one way to remove a behavior.)
> • Use those little claw mittens on each claw. (They do work, although Cheetah takes them off with his teeth.)
> • Only let him have run of the basement, or areas where he cannot destroy things

These will certainly stop destruction due to scratching, but let me also point out: they **DO NOT** teach Cheetah to stop scratching. These steps don't train anything; they just remove an opportunity, which can be an effective and easy fix. The hard part is to successfully remove one opportunity without another taking its place.

The barking dog *(I think this is a pub)*:

This is a very tough one to remove opportunity. It's a natural behavior (as is chewing, digging, and scratching), but while you can take away a slipper, or slip little claw covers on, how do you take away the chance to bark?

• Muzzle Laddie. He won't be able to make sound, but guess what? He's still barking, it just can't come out.
• De-bark him. This is a surgical cutting of the vocal cords. At this point I will take sides and tell you to give Laddie to me first. All you end up with is a barking dog that can't make sounds come out. Easy fix, but a cruel one.
• Lock him in a soundproof room.

As you can tell, avoidance works great in some situations, but is often very difficult to actually implement.

2. Selective Bridging

Another approach to handling self-reinforcing behaviors is to say "good" when the animal is **NOT** taking the opportunity to perform unwanted behavior.

Basically spend a lot of time bridging and reinforcing the animals when they **ARE** doing what you want, which means automatically that they are not doing those other fun behaviors.

Ignore the undesired behavior but reinforce the desired behavior.

Sounds like our basic key to training, doesn't it? In some cases, you also can actually train behaviors that make it physically impossible to do the unwanted behavior. But this has some of the same drawbacks as using punishment effectively. What can you do when you are not present?

By the way, selective bridging is also an excellent way to refine, or "shape" behaviors, and to "scan" new behaviors. Plus, it is one of the most fun and challenging ways to train. Now that I've piqued your interest, we'll talk about it later on.

3. Put the behavior on S^d and then never ask for it except in a session

I'm not sure I'd try this, but it is a method used by some. I question its success. An example is teaching Laddie to "speak" or bark when you give the S^d, and then only ask for the behavior in sessions. The theory is that once you have trained the behavior, Laddie will only do it when asked. But what happens if a cute lady dog walks by, or someone breaks into your house?

And the classic question was once posed to me. What if you are trying to extinguish a self-mutilating behavior, such as a parrot plucking its feathers. Do you bridge the plucking and put it on S^d? No!

And do you really want some big holes in your back yard, or to sacrifice some really nice furniture in order to put those behaviors on S^d? Again, not! So try it on the barking, but first you might want to wait until I explain "scanning" behaviors later in the book.

4. Negative reinforcement

This is where the animal causes his or her own aversive stimulus and stopping the behavior removes that stimulus, therefore increasing not doing the behavior.
Huh?

Okay, I know that sounds complicated, but remember what negative reinforcement is. Something is subtracted from the environment, which increases the likelihood of a behavior (or likelihood of a behavior other than the undesired one).

Carmakers had to deal with a resistant public when it came to seat belts. No one liked, or remembered, to put them on. That is an undesired behavior. So they introduced an annoying buzzing noise that sounds until you put on the seat belt.

Removal of that aversive stimulus (the buzzing noise) increased the likelihood of putting on a seat belt. So if you have an aversive that is paired with the presentation of an unwanted behavior, can you use negative reinforcement to get rid of that behavior? Yep.

Now there are many other ways to get rid of unwanted behaviors, but we are trying to find something that works not only with self-reinforcing behaviors, but also when you are not there to have any input.

A cat's scratch

Let's take scratching as our first example. Now don't leave your basics behind. Simplify, just like you did for figuring out how to train a behavior, and use the same thought process to get rid of one.

Is scratching the behavior you want to get rid of? Or is scratching furniture what you want to get rid of? The second is probably more likely, as scratching is natural and helps cats maintain their claws.

And remember what we were just talking about. The key is not accidentally reinforcing when he does scratch (like shouting, "Hey, quit that!") It may sound like a reprimand to you, but any response can be reinforcing, and won't diminish the reinforcing the cat is getting all on its own. Now you just need to find a way to satisfy the need to scratch, make it positive, and keep it away from Dad's recliner.

Let's look at some of our options.

<u>Option 1</u>

Cut his paws off. Okay, this would be major avoidance. This has been threatened to my cats several times as they attempt to destroy furniture, but somehow they don't take it seriously.

<u>Option 2</u>

Use "selective bridging." Bridge and reinforce Cheetah when he is just hanging out and <u>not scratching</u>. Also, bridge and reinforce when he scratches something he is allowed to scratch, like a scratching post, or whatever you want to use. This is simply blowing the whistle at the right time.

If Cheetah is sitting quietly in your living room, bridge and reinforce his calm behavior. Put a scratching post in a place commonly frequented by Cheetah, and selectively bridge when he uses it. This doesn't mean you have to sit around waiting for it, but you should have your whistle ready (hanging around your neck works for us whale types) and some liver treats in your pocket whenever you are home.

After bridging him for NOT scratching furniture, and bridging him for scratching something else, you will hopefully create a more positive reinforcement around the post and leaving the furniture alone. Then you simply approximate that scratching post to a room where it doesn't have to compete with your fine furniture.

Some would say teaching Cheetah to scratch at all also teaches him he can scratch the furniture. Much like the old theory that if you give a dog a chew-toy, he learns to chew and will chew anything. I beg to differ.

Selective bridging is very powerful and animals will learn which is fun and which isn't. But we still have a problem. Scratching is fun all by itself whether you don't reinforce it or not. So you have a good start.

Option 3

Use "negative reinforcement." Introduce an aversive stimulus that you can pair with the scratching. The key is making it Cheetah's idea to stop scratching and have the aversive stimuli go away.

You could electrify the couch, but then your significant other may be trained not to go near it as well.

Try a squirt gun. Keep it with you when you are around the scratching area, and when Cheetah starts to scratch, squirt him. Don't forget the TIMING! If you squirt too late, you are just getting him wet and he won't know why. That would be punishment, and ineffective punishment, as you really just squirted him for STOPPING scratching. This would be a tad counter-productive.

So what are we doing by squirting him while he scratches and stopping as soon as he stops scratching? When he scratches, water magically hits him, and when he stops (key issue, he stops rather than you stopping him), the water stops. He causes the subtraction of an aversive stimulus, which increases the likelihood that he will stop scratching.

Cool, huh? And again, how you carry out this option is key. If you blow Cheetah across the room with a water cannon, he may never come into the room again.

You want your message clear. "STOP SCRATCHING AND THE WATER STOPS," not "I'm getting you back for scratching, you little weasel"

Pair these two options together and you get a cat that thinks scratching furniture automatically causes a stream of water to hit it, but finds that scratching a post is quite enjoyable. (And those little claw mittens can't hurt either.)

Hot digging dog

This is a very tough behavior to get rid of. One theory for a convenient way to avoid dogs digging in the same spot is to bury their own "poop scoop" results in the hole. *(I have tried this and it sort of seemed to work, but my yard gained a new smell all its own. The grass never did very well, and it certainly didn't stop the behavior. We just get lots more holes.)*

And, again, this behavior is a natural one, and very self-reinforcing.

Option 1

Avoidance. Only let Skipper out when you are with him. Keep him in the house most of the day. This is fine if you have a designated dog area that he lives in, or if you have at least one human that stays at home. Many apartment dwellers practice this without even knowing it and it will certainly keep your dog from digging. But what about those of us who have yards, and want a place for our dogs to run and play, whether we are home or not?

Option 2

Selective Bridging. Same idea as with Cheetah. Create other areas in the yard for Skipper to play in. Play with him, bridge and reinforce him for digging in a sand box you have for him, or for going through tires you place in the yard *(kind of like an obstacle course, or "doggie play set")*.

If you create a fun environment for him, AND you make it even more positive through training, you increase the chances of him doing that instead of digging.

An alternative behavior you could encourage (although you won't need to bridge and reinforce) is chewing on a big old bone, or a rawhide. He can't dig while he's working on a bone. And I have yet to meet a dog that would rather bury a bone than eat it.

This is again teaching him a behavior that is incompatible with the undesired behavior. But we still have a problem with going away all day, and leaving him in the yard. Is your "fun area" as reinforcing as digging? Probably not. So we look back at Cheetah, and jump to:

Option 3

Pair an "aversive" with digging. I'm not sure he'd find a squirt gun aversive. You could try a squirt with a hose. Remember, make it Skipper's idea to stop digging, which stops the aversive stimuli. If you could find a way to run a slight electrical current an inch under the grass, and market it as "no-dig," you could retire almost instantly! Many of you are saying, "That is punishment." Actually, it would be negative reinforcement.

Skipper starts to dig and an aversive stimulus is presented (he gets a mild shock). He makes the decision to stop digging and removes the aversive, increasing the behavior of not digging. (By the way, this is the exact principle as shock collars that are designed to teach a dog to stop barking.)

Just like with scratching cats, you increase the likelihood of Skipper stopping the digging behavior by subtracting the aversive himself. And again, this is not your chance to get even and blast Skipper into his own hole with a pressure washer. He is just doing what comes naturally, but that doesn't mean you can't train him to do something else instead.

Quiet, you stupid mutt

This seems very hard, and I haven't actually trained it. My dogs aren't big barkers. So how do we get rid of a behavior as natural as talking is to humans? My suggestion would be exactly as we trained the other two, and add a twist.

Option 1

Avoidance. Lock him in a room at night and then he only wakes you up, not the whole neighborhood. This certainly is effective for everyone, but you. You could muzzle or cut his vocal cords (ugh), but he's still doing the behavior. So on to:

Option 2

Selective bridging. Bridge and reinforce when he is <u>not</u> barking, especially when he stops for a while after a barking spree. (Be careful not to bridge immediately when he stops or you'll be saying "good job" for all that nice barking.)

He'll soon learn that not barking is often reinforced. (Maybe he will also think sitting without doing anything is what you are reinforcing him for, but it doesn't matter what he is thinking because he is not barking!). And let's toss in some of:

Option 3

Negative reinforcement. Whether a hose, or a squirt gun, pair something with the bark that stops when he stops. Again, <u>he</u> makes the decision to stop barking, which stops the aversive, which is reinforcing the not-barking stuff. The previously mentioned collars may work, but I've never tried one. They may seem a bit harsh, but they are really just another way of using negative reinforcement. The problem is that people tend to just leave them on and not use them as a training tool but as a convenience.

And for an added twist:

Option 4

Train the "bark" behavior. Paired with all the other methods, having the barking on S^d may not be a way to get rid of it, but is an outlet for the natural barking behavior. This is where scanning, and using selective bridging come into play in training a new behavior: to find a consistent way to encourage Laddie to bark.

That might be howling yourself, or waiting until he barks at something else. Bridge it! And reinforce, and encourage or wait for it again. Bridge it and reinforce it. Soon he'll start trying out a bark to see if it gets bridged, and so you start introducing your S^d. When he's into the cycle of giving a "woof," getting bridged, etc., sneak a "speak" S^d into the cycle right after your reinforcement and before he has a chance to offer his bark again. This is called "scanning a behavior."

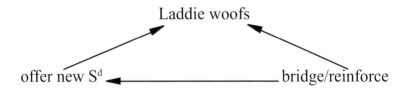

It seems backwards, but look at the diagram. You are "capturing" a behavior without shaping it, and then fitting in an S^d. Soon you'll have your behavior just by using your bridge. And not only is it scanning but also training through selective bridging. By "scanning," we trained lags (short for *Lagenorhynchus obliquiden*s, or Pacific white-sided dolphins) to do high jumping corkscrews, 25-foot high breaches (where whales or dolphins leap up and come crashing back down on their sides), 30-foot leaps, back flips, and to make several different sounds, just like teaching Laddie to "speak."

Now all of that combined should help Laddie stop baying at the moon, or at the neighbor. But if you want to train him on staying quiet when you are not there, how about a remote S^d? You already have trained most of this. Don't believe me? Let's look at the behavior

1. Sit quietly for several minutes on S^d. Didn't we already train a sit-stay or a down-stay? And extend it for longer periods of time?

2. Fade in a second S^d. You've done that several times. All you have to do is figure out an S^d you can give when you are not there. *(Huh?)* What if we fade in a telephone ring as your sit-stay S^d? When the phone rings, Laddie takes the S^d and goes into the behavior. Wow, you trained a complex remote behavior just using some basics. Two problems should be popping up in your head.

    1. How do I bridge?
    2. How do I reinforce?

    These are very good questions. You are coming along well! The answer is, you can't. But you can work the behavior in sessions far more often than actually using it from afar, and that means he will get bridged and reinforced more often than not. This should maintain the behavior. *(You are using variable reinforcement and keeping Laddie on his toes...er...paws.)*

Chapter 13: Oh, that's just his way of saying hello.

Self-reinforcing behaviors are hard to fix. Animals left to their own devices find cool games to play, whether you like the result of the game or not.

Many other problem behaviors are much easier to fix. Why? Because there is a very good chance you have trained them to do that unwanted behavior. I know you didn't mean to, but poor bridging, or something going on during a bridge that you don't see, can teach your animal "superstitious behaviors." Pet owners have a long list of problem behaviors that they think just came out of the blue, but really, most of them are very well-trained. Often by accident!

The first step to solving these problems is recognizing what is happening. Trouble-shooting is a key element in training. As we keep saying, never assume it's the animal. Always assume it's the trainer. When you pay very close attention to a problem behavior, you may see something you've not noticed before, and you're on your way to fixing it.

Let's jump right into some examples and how we might fix them.

Problem Behavior #1

Skipper jumps up on your mother-in-law, planting two muddy paws on her new Ralph Lauren suit. (Didn't we talk about training the dog to let us clean off his paws?) This is a very common behavioral problem.

Why does Skipper rear up and plant his front paws on new guests? It's instinctive? How so? Did his ancestors survive by tackling humans and licking their face until they gave up? I don't think so.

So look at the behavior. What happens when Skipper jumps up on you? Or on any other member of the household? Does he get paid attention to? Do people say, "Hi Skipper, what a good boy"?

Does Skipper get blamed for the ruined clothes, or do you? Can we just admit he gets reinforced every time he rears up and plants his paws on someone's chest? In a very big way? Guess what? You just did some trouble-shooting. The hardest part is recognizing the error; the easy part is fixing it.

Actually, although very easy to fix with Skipper, it's very hard to fix with all those humans. But, either you stop having anyone come to your house *(and no, I don't think that would fly as a good excuse to not having your mother-in-law come over)*, or you need to ask them each and every time to ignore Skipper when he jumps up. Would that, perhaps, be ignoring unwanted behavior?

It is very obvious, upon reflection, that Skipper is being heavily reinforced for the behavior. So remove the reinforcement.

Now, how do you take care of the damage inflicted (and very well trained) up to this point? Try some of the other problem-solving options.

For example, pair an aversive that Skipper will want to get rid of. I have found that dogs like to jump up, but they don't like to be made to stay up, so what if you hold his paws once he jumps up? This was not part of his plan! When he tries to tug free and get back down, don't let him right away.

Again, he makes the choice to jump up, and runs into an aversive stimuli, which, when he drops back down, is removed. By staying down, he removes that weird owner person holding his paws while he was just trying to jump up and plant one on the mom-in-law. By not jumping up, that doesn't happen, so the behavior of not jumping up is increased through negative reinforcement.

Problem behavior #2

You can't get Tex to open his mouth and take the bit, and your riding lesson starts in five minutes! You offer him a carrot and he opens his mouth, and you slip the bit in while he is chewing. You might be thinking, "Hey, I just reinforced him for taking the bit." But did you?

Actually, you just reinforced him holding his mouth shut until you gave him a carrot. You're not training Tex; he is training you.

So how do you fix it? Well, first make sure that anyone who tacks up Tex follows whatever guideline you are going to use. Consistency is extremely important any time there is more than one trainer involved. When you are working by yourself, you don't need to worry about it as much. You still need to be consistent, but it's pretty easy to be consistent with yourself!

Now that you know what is happening, and can recognize the behavior you have accidentally trained, it is fairly easy to fix. Since you have already taught Tex the bridge and all, now you just need to bridge the behavior you <u>do</u> want, which is opening his mouth on S^d, rather than baiting it open with food.

So when you don't have the bit, or aren't getting ready to ride, do some quick sessions on just opening his mouth. With a dolphin, we could just open their mouth with our fingers and bridge, and we had not only a behavior, but an S^d as well.

If Tex doesn't let you open his mouth manually (and you don't want to bridge him resisting opening his mouth), use whatever "trick" you normally use to put in the bit. Some people press on the corner of the mouth where the joint of the jaws is. Either way, encourage him to open his mouth (you may as well pair your S^d "mouth" right away each time you are asking) and when he does, bridge. That's all there is to it.

Once he has the behavior during those little sessions, introduce the bit as a variable in the session, but should you try to put it in right away? If you said "nope," good job! You just want to desensitize him to it, and then work it into the sessions up to where you put it in after asking for a "mouth-open." Then work it into the schedule for when you actually need him to wear the bit.

But don't forget to do those sessions without riding. This is just another game, and you shouldn't only play it when you need it, but rather all the time.

Again, try to simplify. When you have a problem behavior, look at all the variables, and how and when you are bridging and how and when you reinforce. Remember the bouncing dog syndrome when you asked for a "sit," and can't figure out why Laddie bounces right back up? He is getting bridged for it, right as he gets up, rather than right as he sits. Once you spot that, you just change your TIMING. There it is again. The importance of timing.

Think back to some of those pitfalls in training "retrieval." If you accidentally bridge a few times when Skipper tugs at the Frisbee rather than handing it to you, that tug of war is something you trained through inadvertent bridging.

If Tex is kicking the door of the trailer as you close it, is he mad? Or did you just not notice that your bridge for staying on target also happened to bridge him for kicking out at the same time?

Sometimes, an animal does something extra along with the behavior you are trying to bridge, and you get that unwanted extra behavior, as well. (It's not Skipper's fault - you bridged it.) Those are "superstitious behaviors," and again, the key is recognizing where they came from and getting rid of the errant bridges or reinforcements.

That is why being selective with your bridge is so important. Remember, Skipper, Laddie, Cheetah, and Tex don't know what you want to bridge, they just remember what they were doing <u>when</u> you bridged. And that might not be the behavior you wanted!

Chapter 14: Selective bridging to improve behaviors, not just to fix them

This is really fun training! Just like extending targets, you can teach a great deal by just using your whistle. No targets, just blowing the whistle at an exact moment can "shape" behavior as effectively as a target-training.

Working with Pacific white-sided dolphins gives us lots of good examples. Just by using the bridge, we could get maximum speed (up to 30-mph!) out of one of our dolphins and more than 20-foot leaps out of another. Training the behavior itself doesn't accomplish this, but good selective bridging can take the behavior up several notches.

So if we can train a lag (Pacific white-sided dolphin) to jump higher and swim faster, then couldn't we train a horse to do the same?

Most riders would not think of a bridge as a means to improve a horse's performance, but if you are in a cross-country event, what if you could get your horse to improve the speed and height of a jump while you were actually in the event? You can, through selective bridging. So let's see how…

You could encourage the horse with a racing or riding crop, which certainly works (and could be either negative reinforcement or positive punishment depending on how it is used) or you could use a bridge. Remember that a key element in a bridge is the ability to say "good job" and reinforce later. In this case, we would probably be reinforcing with a "secondary" or non-food item, as it's pretty hard to give a carrot to a horse at 25-mph.

But you can give them a pat on the neck, and don't forget that the bridge itself is a very strong secondary reinforcer, as normally it is followed by a primary. You have already trained Tex with a verbal secondary when training "trailer," so now just use the same means to train a pat on the neck as a solid secondary.

Remember, don't assume Tex likes a quick pat on his neck, or a scratch between the ears. Train it, just like you did when you were working on Tex going into the trailer.

You know what the behavior is going to be (increasing his speed), so you want to pick something you feel is reinforcing (which you can guess from the "relationship" you have formed…remember?). This can be a word in his ear, an ear scratch, or a pat on the neck.

Now make sure it is reinforcing. Just as you did before, pat his neck and while you do, bridge and reinforce! Guess what? After several times, the pat means bridge which means primary and you have another secondary reinforcer (to go along with the word "good" from earlier. You can alternate these for variety in your secondaries).

Now you have a reinforcer that you can use while you are riding. Reminder: don't misuse or overuse secondaries without primaries, or pretty soon Tex will be fairly miffed that he doesn't get a carrot. All of a sudden, your secondary becomes aversive and you might find yourself lofting through the air, wondering where the horse formerly underneath you disappeared to.

So it is a good idea to intersperse secondaries with primaries, and use both at times. When Tex targets his leg up for hoof-cleaning, you bridge, pat him on the neck, and give him a carrot.

To get your horse to go faster as you are riding, go into a gallop, and when Tex seems to be at a high speed, bridge and pat for reinforcement. Something you might experience is a bit of confusion at the bridge, at which point the horse might pull up to see what he did right, and where his carrot might be. In that case, do not reinforce. NEVER reinforce a bad bridge, and never reinforce if the animal does something you don't want before you have the chance to reinforce. Simply wait a second, get started again, and try again. He'll get it quickly.

Now, once you feel you have bridged him for going what feels like a certain speed a few times, get him started again and, this time, don't bridge when he first reaches that speed. Wait until he has been at the speed for five seconds; then the next time wait for seven seconds, and so on.

What do you think Tex will do? He'll speed up even more! The thought process could sound something like "Hey, where's the bridge? Wait, I'll go faster; maybe I wasn't going fast enough!"

Tex is trying to get that bridge as he is running. Each time you feel he has settled in at a certain speed, try to move up again. Soon, just by bridging, you end up at Tex's top speed without a whip or a crop, and Tex and you are likely having a blast.

Don't forget his natural characteristics. You're not going to get him up to 60-mph. And don't forget to back up that secondary reinforcer with primaries (carrots) when you're done. You can do this by the ol' pat-bridge-reinforce, or by simply doing both after working another behavior. Remember to always do the secondary ("pat"), then the primary (carrot) 'cuz Tex won't care much about the pat right after he gets that carrot.

The exact process is also true with jumping. Simply bridge at a starting height and then approximate (by not bridging until he goes a bit higher) up!

Now lots of you are thinking about stuff you've done for years that seems to work, or about how your dog likes a pat better than hot dogs, or your horse understands the crop...etc, etc. No arguments here, because I can't tell you the opposite with any more proof than you can give me.

My point is not that dogs don't like a tummy rub, or that horses don't like a pat on the neck. My point is why not make sure? Training is most effective when you are very clear with the animal; clear on what you are asking for, clear in saying "good job," and very clear in a positive result.

Be sure your reinforcer is positive or the training won't work. In fact, that is a heck of a troubleshooting point. What are you reinforcing? How are you reinforcing?

Ever seen a dog avoid a pat on the head from someone it doesn't know? Could it be because of the learned relationship with its owner/trainer rather than a natural love of being petted? The entire relationship is learned.

An example of this is that annoying "kissie" noise a lot of people make around animals. You know the noise I mean, where they rub their fingers together and make that noise, assuming the animal will come over? As a dolphin trainer, it is annoying to watch people hang over railings and do that to the whales and dolphins.

Why do they do it? Because that is how their dog comes over. So do all animals come at that noise? Or did Rover learn that when his owner makes that noise and he comes over, he gets reinforced? We tell people over and over again that the whales and dolphins couldn't care less about that noise and that they certainly don't respond to it. This was because they were never taught to, and your dog was, whether you realize it or not. Your relationship with your animal is entirely learned.

Animals don't automatically like certain things. Even if a tummy rub feels good, they may not like it from your two-year-old, who takes out a lot of fur at the same time. So it never hurts to train that part of the relationship when using it in more formal training.

So now we have learned some basic animal training ideas, like bridging, targeting, timing, ignoring unwanted behavior, and breaking down training into simple concepts. And that is all we have used so far!

No complicated props, electronic beepers, cattle prods, special collars and chains. Just training, just spending four times a day working with your personal "whale with fur."

Now training can go to some very complicated levels, and there is a veritable alphabet soup of terms, initials, and slang. You can use variable schedules of reinforcement, differential reinforcement, random intermittent reinforcement, least-reinforcing stimulus, chained behaviors, behavior streams, streams of consciousness, and streams of beer. Okay, so I'm a little off track. It is page 126 after all! The point is, unless you are a professional trainer *(and won't need this book)* you really don't have the time, or need, to learn and use all these tools. The basics will do you just fine.

For example, we can use all the basics to train some important veterinary behaviors. In fact, you probably already have.

One way to go to the vet, at least for a wild beluga whale.

Chapter 15: Yippee, going to the vet!

Let's take Skipper to the vet. Sound familiar? Sounds just like loading Tex on a trailer, except for the potential destination. But still, most people will claim Skipper KNOWS when he is going to the vet. In reality, it is far more likely that he knows the car ride is going to end in something negative. It is very unlikely that Skipper's brain comes up with, "Wow, that lady is getting her purse, putting the children in the car, and now is coming towards me…my goodness, we must be embarking to the veterinary office, where I might be stuck upon the rump with a sharp needle…I know…I'll run away!" More likely, Skipper thinks "CAR = BAD PLACE."

You could actually compare this to going to the dentist for you. Just the note in your appointment book can give you shivers, whether it's just a routine cleaning, or more. This is because doctor and dentist appointments were rarely made positive. Parents often say, "Oh no, I have to go to the dentist," which is what the kids hear, and they assume it is bad news.

My wife and I started taking our kids with us to the dentist very early in their lives and they got to sit in the chair, and play in the office, and look at all the shiny tools. Now, they all like going to the dentist. We made it a game! And they played that game fairly often compared to when they really need to go for a procedure.

Another great example of how training can help out is by taking a look at the old zoo adage that says that all the animals in the zoo hate the veterinarian on sight. This is quite often true. Every time they see the vet wandering near them something bad happens (injections, darts, physical restraint, pills, etc).

But the vets at every place I've worked have never experienced that! Why? Because every thing we did was made into a training game. We played those games all the time. When I went to Ocean Journey, the vet (already an experienced marine mammal guy) was all prepared for the tigers to act aggressively whenever he was around. Four years later, however, they still treated him as just another one of us trainers, simply because we taught them that.

So how does all of this help you with Skipper? Well, remember how we taught the dolphins to transport? Or Tex to go into the trailer? Same idea, just forget where you want to take Skipper.

First, simplify the behavior. Do you want Skipper to go to the vet? Sure you do, but don't you have a simpler behavior to look at? That's right - just going for a ride in the car. So how do we start?

Option 1

Put Skipper's leash on him, and drag him to the car, pick him up, shove him in the back seat, and shut the door. *(On the way to the vet, you might want to stop by the car wash and get the interior scrubbed, because Skipper is a little freaked out.)*

Option 2

How about just teaching Skipper to get into the car? And let's start with our trusty friend, the target!

A target pole would be easier here, and you can use Tex's target pole or make a smaller one. (A nylaball on a small dowel works great.) Just target Skipper at the open door, bridge (whistle), and reinforce (hot dog piece). Target his nose (don't ask him to jump up right away) inside the door opening, bridge, reinforce.

Take small steps, approximate to where Skipper is comfortable with the target and leaning into the car. Then target him so that he has to put his front feet into the car to reach the target.

Just keep working until Skipper is all the way in, and then bridge and reinforce just for being calm in the car. (I would teach him to climb in on the floor of the front seat to allow easy reinforcement as you progress.) Soon Skipper should be sitting calmly on the floor of your car.

While Skipper is sitting in the car, don't forget to occasionally bridge and reinforce him for being calm. While doing this, start the car, and if Skipper stays calm (including demeanor, not just staying still) bridge and reinforce). You can progress from this to short rides, always bridging calm behavior during your progression.

Pretty soon you can drive just about anywhere and Skipper will be happy with it. Remember to take drives, just as a game, and don't automatically start going to the vet, or the groomer. <u>You want to play the game at least three times as often as actually doing the behavior</u> (going to the vet).

Now for the veterinarian part. It can be hard, because a small animal vet probably won't be able to have you stop by a few times a week to get the dog desensitized to the office or the vet. But, using the very same methods we used to teach Skipper to like a car ride, you can make the front step and the waiting room positive experiences.

When the car rides reach the vet's office, reinforce well for just parking in the lot. Let Skipper out, and reinforce him for getting out of the car. In other words, use the tools you already have, like targeting, bridging, and TIMING, to teach Skipper the vet's office is a fun, fun place.

Remember that all behaviors need fixing at times, and the one time Skipper does go to the vet for real, you can't make the actual shot fun (or can you?), so you might have to regress a bit and teach him again after the visit.

Regression, or going back a step or two, is a normal part of training, and will usually only require a few quick reminders on some of the steps.

But hold on! Let's go back to the part about not being able to make the shot fun. Didn't I say you could teach just about anything to be positive? So can we make a shot fun? Sure we can!

Let's assume Tex needs a cortisone shot once a week. As always, think about the behavior and what it really is. Is it an injection or is it standing still while variables happen around him? Right, it is standing still and staying calm no matter what's going on, including a needle going into his skin.

In Tex's mind, does he know, except by past experience, what an injection is? To him, he just has to stand still while something pinches him. So the basic behavior is to be calm and hold still while he gets pinched. Now break it down into simple steps.

Whales with Fur

Chapter 16: Hey, whatcha doin' with that needle?

Let's jump right in…

<u>Option 1</u>

Stand next to his shoulders…lean against the stall for support…aim, close your eyes…and JAB! *(When you regain consciousness, peel yourself off the wall of the stall, and see if you can find Tex).*

<u>Option 2</u>

Teach Tex to stand calmly for extended periods of time. And if you remember, you have already trained that with Skipper. It's just stationing. With whales, we called it "parallel stationing," because we taught them to float parallel to the deck we (the trainers) were working from.

They were trained to stay in that position calmly while we rolled them over, or picked up their tail, or checked out their eyes, or took a blowhole sample, or stuck them with a needle.

If "stationing" for Tex is facing you (perpendicular to you) in the stall, then teach him a parallel station against one wall, or have him do an extended target on a fixed wall target (this helps focus attention AWAY from any needles or probing or tubes).

Make sure you have that simple starting point trained. Once you have him in a parallel station and staying there until you bridge, you are ready to move on.

Next, desensitize Tex to being "manipulated" while in his parallel, or quiet, station. Ask for stationing, or an extended target, and rub your hand along his side, then bridge. After you reinforce, put him back into parallel station, and approximate to greater times and more rubbing, lifting of his legs, etc.

In fact, this lengthened parallel station is a great way to train Tex to hold still for a variety of husbandry (care) behaviors, like combing out his tail, or brushing him down, or picking out his hooves. And you end up bridging and reinforcing calm stationing throughout even simple behaviors, like brushing. That will make it all the easier to train something like a "needle stick."

Once you are up to a minute or two, and Tex is holding still while you prod him, rub him, etc., try poking him gently with your finger at the future injection point. If he stays calm, bridge at that same moment you poke him. Don't forget to vary those "manipulations," making his accepting new and different stimuli part of the game.

Timing is also important. Sometimes bridge during the manipulation, and sometimes bridge the calm stationing after several pokes and prods.

You want to keep doing that until he really doesn't seem to care that this little biped thing is poking his shoulder. Then try something a bit sharper, like a paper clip. Eventually progress (through small approximations) to a pin *(sterilize it first, please)* and actually poke the skin and bridge. As you continue to progress, Tex won't care what you're doing, he's just waiting for that bridge.

Now you need to introduce some new variables. Are you giving the injections? Probably not; so don't assume Tex will hold still with two people there instead of one. You don't need the vet's help specifically, just grab whomever is nearby, and train their presence as a new variable.

Take a step back and, while Tex is in the parallel station, introduce the second person next to you *("Tex, this is Joe. Joe, this is Tex." Only kidding)*.

Rather, bridge calm stationing with a second person present, and approximate to the point where your "vet stand-in" does some of the tactile stimuli, the rubbing etc. Once Tex seems comfortable, simply continue as before with your second person doing the poking and prodding. Even if you are going to give your own injection, training for a second person can help out with the blacksmith, vet, baths, etc.

Once you've bridged and reinforced your way to a calm horse, no matter what or who is poking around, and you continuously play this game as part of each training session, then you are done!

The vet's just another second person, the needle is just part of the game, whether there's an actual injection or not, and Tex is trained to stand still and be calm until you bridge.

So you <u>can</u> train your dog, cat, horse, or pot-bellied pig to think a shot is fun. And what's the basic behavior? <u>Staying at station calmly</u>.

That's pretty much it. The rest is just approximated into stationing in small steps. But just in case you think you can't train things like needles and vets to be positive, let me share a few experiences with you.

We once trained a Pacific white-sided dolphin that needed daily injections to float in a parallel station while he received an injection three times a day. Keep in mind, the needle had to be long enough to go through skin, blubber layer, and into the muscle tissue. We used about a three-inch needle, and he did the behavior every day for a long time.

We also trained a dolphin with kidney stones to accept a stomach tube while at station (dolphins and whales have no gag reflex) and then we would give her a liter of water to help with the kidneys. We did this four times a day. Now remember, you can't make a dolphin stay with you for a session unless it wants to!

A harbor seal developed pneumonia. We taught her to wear a respirator mask four times a day so we could introduce a fine medicated mist into her lungs. *(This was pretty cute to watch. She looked like a little seal "pilot.")*

We taught the whales to let us pump milk when they were pregnant so we could store some, learn about its composition, and use it for future calves, if needed.

All the animals were taught to urinate on S^d so we could take a sample. *(Now if I could just teach my kids that!)*

We could do fecal samples, blowhole swabs, and have the animals blow forcibly into a Petri dish so we could check out their lungs.

We did ultrasounds, x-rays, weighings, eye exams, and gastric samples.

Some animals have been trained to allow endoscopies, catheterization, oral surgery, and even cauterizing, all in part of a training session, cooperating with the trainer!

And that's just the cooperative or veterinary behaviors. Then there are all those fun, wild behaviors you see when you go to a marine park, or an oceanarium.

So it can be done, and now you have the tools to do it, too.

I hope you've found that any behavior you want to train, or any behavior you want to fix, can be analyzed, broken down, and trained very simply. Just rely on the basic tools you have learned here, and you can train almost anything.

Even better is the relationship you develop with your animal, whether it is a dog, horse, or cat. Some of my best friends are beluga whales and Pacific-white-sided dolphins. It's just a big, wonderful game you teach them, and one they like to play.

So go out there and have fun with your very own whales with fur!

Index

Photographic Credits
(Listed by Page Number)

Cover	Shannon Cremeans/Marineland of Florida/ Pete Davey
iii	Lisa Takaki
1	Shannon Cremeans/Marineland of Florida
2	Pete Davey
3	Johanna Davey
4	Ed Lines, Jr./Shedd Aquarium
5	Ed Lines, Jr./Shedd Aquarium (top picture)
5	Lisa Takaki (bottom picture)
6	Pete Davey
7	Scott Dressel-Martin
8	Shannon Cremeans/Marineland of Florida
9	Pete Davey
11	Johanna Davey
23	Johanna Davey
26	Pete Davey
29	Johanna Davey
39	Shannon Cremeans/Marineland of Florida
47	Lisa Takaki
55	Pete Davey
57	Pete Davey
67	Pete Davey
83	Shannon Cremeans/Marineland of Florida
87	Pete Davey
91	Pete Davey
121	Shannon Cremeans/Marineland of Florida
127	Pete Davey
133	Johanna Davey
138	Ed Lines, Jr./Shedd Aquarium

Illustration Credits

About the Author

Pete Davey has been involved in advanced animal training and care for 16 years. He has worked with whales, dolphins, sea lions, seals, sea otters, river otters, tigers, and birds. Pete also has taught trainers throughout his career. He is currently the Director of Training for Marineland of Florida, and is working on his second book, *A Dolphin in Front of You,* a pocket guide to becoming an animal trainer. Pete lives in Florida with his wife, Jody, and their four children: Kelsey, Ty, Sam, and Kate. (And, of course, with Cheetah, Skipper, Laddie, and Alger.)

Ocean Publishing
Quick Order Form

Fax orders: 386-517-2564. <u>Send this completed form.</u>
Telephone orders: Call 888-690-2455 toll free in USA.
Have your credit card ready.
E-mail orders: orders@ocean-publishing.com
Postal orders: Ocean Publishing, Orders Department, P.O. Box 1080, Flagler Beach, Florida 32136-1080, USA.
Telephone 386-517-1600.

Please send me the following order of *Whales with Fur, How to train any animal using Dolphin training techniques*

<u>Quantity</u>	<u>Price/Book</u>	<u>$Total</u>	
_____	**$14.95 Softcover**	$ _____	(USA)
	Sales Tax*	$ _____	
	Shipping**	$ _____	
	Order Total	$ _____	

***Sales Tax:** Add 7% for orders to Florida addresses
****Shipping:** Add $3.45 for first book and $1.85 for each additional book.

Payment Method: **Check** (# of enclosed check_____)
Credit Card   __Visa   __Mastercard   __Discover
Card Number: _____ Exp. Date: _____
Name on card: _____

Name: _____
Street/P.O. Box: _____
City: _____ State: ___ Zip: _____
Telephone: (___) - _____ E-mail: _____

Please send free information about:

❏ Other books   ❏ Author speaking
❏ Author Events